AWAKENING STARSEEDS

SHATTERING ILLUSIONS VOL. 1

CURATED BY RADHAA NILIA

Copyright @ 2019 **Awakening Starseeds**™ 1st Edition

Copyright @ 2021 **Awakening Starseeds**™ 2nd Edition

All Rights Reserved

ISBN: 978-1-952124-00-6

CONTENTS

DEDICATION

Dedicated to Starseeds around the World.

FOREWORD

By Maya The Shaman

Awakening Starseeds: Shattering Illusions (Volume 1) is a multidimensional weaving of real-life stories from all walks of life. This book contains raw and revealing incidents, honest, real-life experiences by authors who openly and shamelessly share their trapped and hidden life stories. These stories, once-upon-a-time stored in darkness, are here allowed to surface into the light.

Each author offers their inner strength and courage, sharing vulnerabilities from an authentic place. These offerings are real gifts that will heal our world. The result is their victory of embodying their voices through storytelling. You, too, can transmute your darkness into light. These awakening stories will link and act as a bridge to other Starseeds awakening at this time.

Like the beautiful lotus flower, Starseeds must emerge from the deepest depths. A lotus struggles through the murky darkness and mud yet moves upwards to grow until it reaches the surface. Despite having to live in darkness, the lotus is untouched by the mud. It opens gracefully above the mud; its petals have an unstoppable momentum to meet the light. This book, Awakening Starseeds: Shattering Illusions, Volume I, is just like this lotus flower. From darkness to light, we go.

Thank you for reading my foreword.

In Love, Light, and Namaskar.
　　Salamat Po,
　　Maya The Shaman

INTRODUCTION

I was divinely inspired to create a collaborative book series for Starseeds voices from around the world. We did not know what to expect. And when we asked, "Who wants to be a part of this?" The response was incredible.

For the first run of Awakening Starseeds, our tribe responded from far and wide. People heard the call from Asia, Europe, Canada, and of course, the United States. We were blown away by these beautiful souls that entrusted us to share their voices, their messages, and their own stories as a Starseeds family.

The Universe had divinely assigned us to show up, and when we did, they showed up too. We hope you will find some inspiration from these stories and that you will remember your sacred calling.

Know you are not alone in these challenging times. We stand in between the age of darkness (Kali Yuga) and light (Satya Yuga). Whenever you may feel at a loss, lonely or alone, remember you have your soul family embracing you. We are, in fact, in this cosmic journey together.

If you are reading this right now, this is a confirmation from the Divine. You have not been forgotten. You are a part of this significant shift as much as anyone else. Indeed, you can make a difference. Most importantly, your voice matters. We are here as conduits to help voices come forth into our world. We offer our support to write your story in a book form as co-authors of the Awakening Starseeds series. We are the change that we want to see in the world. Will you join us?

With devotion to the divine,
    Radhaa

MY STARSEED JOURNEY
REMEMBERING MY PURPOSE

By RADHAA NILIA

A middle-aged woman walked into the gallery and straight towards me. Her long dark hair was flowing to her waist. She appeared to be an indigenous woman. Elegant and timeless in her flowing dress with glowing brown skin and deep brown eyes, she seemed to see straight through me as her soulful eyes lock into mine.

I felt startled by the intensity of her presence before me. I wondered if we had met before. She seemed so familiar, yet I could not place her in my memory. As she glided towards me with a soft smile, I smiled back, mesmerized.

"Welcome to Iris Blossom. How can I help you?" I asked since she seemed to be there on a mission. People often said they were 'drawn' into the store and felt they just had to go in. Once inside, it seemed to awaken their childlike nature full of wonder. I would watch with amusement as their eyes got large as saucers. They looked around as if they had entered a whole other world. "WOW!" They would often mutter, followed by a long pause as they looked around, soaking up all the bright colors.

The energy of the space held the frequency of abundance, creativity, beauty, and healing. The moment anyone walked into the store, their senses were filled with the aromatic essential oils permeating the air. World music played inside and outside the store puts a skip in people's steps.

Visitors from every continent came to celebrate the artistic city of Ashland, Oregon, home of the Shakespeare Festival. We were right across the street from the Shakespeare Theatre so that crowds would rush in droves after the shows.

Inside the store, very long bamboo poles ran across the ceiling. Silk draped from the bamboo poles where colorful hand-painted scarves sat mid-air like a flock of birds, inviting and enchanting.

Salmon-painted walls lined up with the softest and most feminine garments made of silks and sueded rayon presented as wearable arts. Clients often bought hand-painted kimonos to hang on their walls. Each one was one of a kind, rare, and custom-designed.

The process of making a kimono took a significant amount of patience. My mom hand-picked the fabric, washed it, ironed it, and then each piece was hand-cut, ready for stitching. The entire process of creating one kimono could take a week. Soon after the stitching, my mom outlined tropical birds, flowers, or insects on it. Once drawn, it was time to paint on the silk. The process of painting was slow and steady, with great attention to detail for an entire day. And sometimes, we worked into the night.

Each painted garment was unique, special, and imprinted with a specific healing frequency. Each infused to bring about an energy signature as it called to the right customer. These were not any ordinary clothes or art. They were both beautiful and healing adornments. An infusion of healing energy, when chosen, was transferred to the buyer. Women would come back year after year, raving at how good it made them feel, how empowered or beautiful they felt in it.

Power totems. We loved our creations. We worked with the divine, and the divine worked with us. The reward was in our clients experiencing newfound confidence, joy, gratitude, and coming back year after year as our soulmate clients.

My mom would walk around the store early in the morning before anyone came by. She would take her time to touch, pray, and bless each jewelry case, the racks, the garments, and infuse it with her heart. Everything vibrated with the mantra of love.

It happened to be one of these mornings, just after my mom had blessed everything in the store, that this mysterious woman walked in, stopped, right in front of me. "I need to talk to you," I looked around—no one else here but my mom, who was busy getting ready for the day. I looked back at her, like, what? "Of course, how can I help you!"

"You have a large and masculine guide that stands behind you. Your guardian and protector." I looked behind me but did not see anything. Huh? I wondered if she was perhaps crazy as she proceeded. "I am here to share a special message with you about your future." I got a bit of a chill. I had not thought much about my future. I just wanted to be in the moment.

"You will be working with the light grid, with teams of healers, innovators, artists, leaders, and Starseeds across the globe in doing this. Your work, along with your team, is most important and vital."

Light grid? What in the holy guacamole was she talking about? I did not know anything about a light grid. A team of people? Very unlikely, as I enjoyed doing things on my own.

I was a bit of an introvert, and there is no way I would have a team of people around me. She continued with the broadest smile as if she was blissed out on cloud nine, informing me. "You have a long way to go, young lady. You will endure a lot before you get there. It's all written in your code." Code? What code is she talking about? I'm not a robot; I'm a human. Humans don't have such Codes, or so I thought. She added you're one of the Starseeds. Starseeds? I am so confused right now.

My eyes must have been squinting at her, trying to understand as she offered: "I am here to help you align your code so that it activates properly at the right time." All I could think was, am I dreaming?

This lady was friendly, warm, and seemed familiar, but what she was saying to me was just beyond my scope of understanding. She continued, nonetheless. "Your energetic code has been compromised through trauma. I am here to assist you in this." I felt like I was amid a sci-fi movie and was the frantic heroine trying to figure out my mission.

"I am going to need to meet with you after work so that I can help reset that for you." She said this all as if she expected me to go along with her. Umm...what?! Meet outside the store? I don't usually meet clients or people outside our store hours. My mom was listening to our conversation, and I saw her turn and smile at us knowingly.

"Why don't you come over at seven pm? I'll give you the address," mom said with a wink. I looked at her with googly eyes, like what!? But there was a part of me that also felt I needed to meet with her.

As much as I wanted her just to be crazy so I could write her off and go on living my healthy life, whatever that means yet, I resonated with what she was saying on a soul level.

Though I had no idea what she was talking about, my soul understood what my ears and mind could not. Somewhere from another life, I knew her. I was curious, nervous, but there was also a part of me that was calm and just accepted that this was a part of my destiny.

The store was funny like that. It brought in people together, destined to meet, and I had more than a few mystics who came and told me things that I did not comprehend but 'needed to share.' They all said it would be critical information. I would appreciate it and understand when it was time.

The doorbell rang, I opened the door of our house, and she was standing there, very sure of her reason for coming. We just smiled at each other, and I let her in. We walked down the hall silently to my bedroom. My stomach was turning inside out with anticipation, and I tried to keep calm.

Once inside my bedroom, she instructed me to lay down. She said she was going to perform some "sort of energy work" on me. I just closed my eyes, relaxed into the experience, and let her lead the way. She called in the galactic council, whatever that meant. I felt the room fill up with something unexplainable. Warmth, energy, beings, family, love surrounded me.

She then told me that my Codes had been damaged. Energy strands are cut off or pulled apart. Holographic inserts implanted to stop me from progressing. I had no concept of what that even meant. She told me I had been taken apart and re-assembled in a different way than was meant to be. Pieces of me, stolen. A lot of induced trauma, as she explained. But I wouldn't be able to remember these traumatic events as my mind had already been erased, yet the well-hidden wounds were still there.

This kind of thing has been happening to people on the planet for thousands of years. I wasn't the only one. Many, many others, were experiencing the same process of interference and distortions.

She said I would have to be very diligent, as these experiments are ongoing. These evil beings tracked every soul before incarnating. They also have a way of knowing which souls have come to be a part of this galactic shift. I had no idea what the galactic shift meant. So why in the world would anyone want to distort me?

She continued to say how these dark beings created artificial problems, programs, trauma, and neural blocks. It has veered many Starseeds far off track, making them susceptible to suicidal thoughts, depression, anxiety, abuse, addictions, self-sabotage, and various destructive self-programs. Sadly, many who heard the clarion call, who came to earth to assist, got so lost in the darkness that they could no longer return to their true nature.

She warned me that it was a marathon and not a sprint. But even if I did forget, she was installing a sort of protective grid inside of me that would keep the integrity of my 'Starseed Code.' I was almost dozing off from her very soothing voice, and this warm feeling of love and safety that was so healing for me was like a lullaby. I felt like a big happy baby.

I no longer cared about what she was saying. I was just in a state of surrender, allowing and letting my subconscious mind record her. I knew that I had a long way to go, many experiences to acquire. Deep down, I trusted when the time was right; I would 'understand' all that she said and trusted her. It all reverberated into my subconscious. Many years passed since then, and I had forgotten the wise words of this woman.

On my journey, I had taken many kinds of paths into the underworld. She was correct in saying that many harmful programs and holograms reinstalled in me since our connection. It only was when I started energy healing work that I began to clear and cleanse myself from these dark energies for good. I had to learn to say NO. To set me free from their programming as part of my path to sovereignty.

Dark beings, in many different forms, visited me. They were trying to reinstall negative grids to stop me from my path. They were very successful for a long time. I was so programmed many things in this world had seduced me. Yet, none led to the happiness promised when sold. I had to undo the damage and gain strength to break up with the toxic cycle.

After years of being filled with fears, I had to face many of them to break free, to stand for my sovereignty. I discovered these beings thought they owned me and my lineage. And I would be the one to break the curses, to go rogue and to step out of line and to reclaim my being. I would release programming which controlled patterns that had ruled me and many in my lineage for so many years.

Through my healing journey, I wrote my book, Memoirs of a Galactic Goddess, Ascending Beyond Duality, to transmute and process the trauma in this lifetime. I am grateful for the many lessons from the experiences I have endured. It was for me to understand the depth of duality truly. To immerse so completely and then find my way out of the cosmic maze.

Part of remembering also to understand how we are in this together. We are indeed a family of light. Our voices united in this book. We may all have different experiences, but somehow, we can weave them all together for a higher purpose. I found that through the power of writing out my life experiences as a human, I also detached and released trauma around them.

Now it's only a story of once upon a time. I am growing and changing every day into a more upgraded version of myself. No one has all the pieces of this puzzle, but all do have a part to contribute. And as we build camaraderie and find relatedness in our experiences, rather than our differences, we can truly embody the new human we are becoming. Awakening Starseeds is for those who are remembering.

Who are ready to come out of the spiritual closet and share their stories of awakening. We are coming together worldwide, proclaiming our sovereignty, finding our voices, and standing with our light for those who seek to see us, and we are here. Will you join us?

In love and gratitude,
Radhaa

ABOUT THE AUTHOR

Radhaa Nilia

Radhaa Nilia is the curator of "Awakening Starseeds" book series. She is a multimedia artist, coach, and teacher. She works with women to activate their inner Goddess, heal their heart and soul wounds to find their higher purpose at Goddess Code Academy™.

Goddess Code Academy™ is a mystical school for the divine feminine where she provides certification programs and teaches her original healing modality called Goddess Activations™.

Radhaa is the founder of Radhaa Publishing House and a contributing writer for various online magazines such a Huffington Post, Elephant Journal, Splash Magazine.

To find Radhaa go to:
www.RadhaaNilia.net

～

2

THE KNOCK

MY LEMURIAN GREAT-GREAT GRANDFATHER

By Maya Verzonilla
As MAYA THE SHAMAN

Two urgent loud knocks at my front door startled me as if those large knuckles belonged to a powerful man who can't wait to deliver a critical message.

Such knocking is not usual or welcome here in the rugged mountains of North Carolina. People here do not like unannounced visits and being bothered.

I live at the very top of one of the Appalachian Mountains, up a long winding, dirt road and a nearly hidden driveway. I wasn't expecting any visitors or deliveries. So, who might this be?

Our dogs barked at the knocking. I reached out to slightly open the front door only to find there's no one! They stopped their barking and began sniffing the patio for whoever it was who knocked.

If anyone may have been playing games with me, there's just no place to hide.

From where I stood, the outdoor space was clear. This is

not possible. I heard the knocks, the dogs heard them too, but no one was there. It gave me a shiver down my spine.

I closed my eyes for a moment to scan my heart and mind. Then a vision came to me. It was Don Pedro, my great-great-grandfather, a Lemurian Shaman in my native land Maharlika, called the Philippines. My father never had a chance to tell me about him. But his mother, my grandmother, Lola Senyang did.

When my Grandma Lola Senyang spoke about Don Pedro, her soft, gentle, serene yet serious voice carried great respect and honor towards him. I can never forget a story told by her. She said:

"Don Pedro traveled to any place or country he desires on his bubble. He did not use a vehicle, a plane, or any other form of transportation. He teleports himself through space and time to his desired destination in spirit time."

––––––––––––

Don Pedro was a Shaman with shape-shifting skills and abilities, a very mysterious man. He had the power to appear and disappear unnoticed and possessed powers out of this 3rd dimension. There are 4th, 5th, and higher dimensions that ordinary human beings have no clue about or understanding when it comes to the spirit realm.

My grandmother continued her story. She said Don Pedro told his family that he was leaving for America that day and would be back in three days. While Don Pedro was gone, several robbers got into his house, packing his precious belongings in their bags. They took the goods and hurried on their way out but got lost in a maze.

To their surprise, they could not find any openings, the door and windows were gone!

Thieves kept going around and around inside Don Pedro's house, only to repeat the same steps, tracing them back where they have already been before. They spent hours after hours and then days searching for that mysteriously lost door, which they never found. It left them exhausted, terrified, and somewhat insane.

It was then that they realized Don Pedro's home was not an ordinary house. They should not have tried to rob it, but it was too late. Don Pedro could change the physical structure of matter. He had closed all the portals of his house and trapped them in. After three days, Don Pedro returned home. The door and windows appeared again.

The police escorted Don Pedro to fetch the robbers. Obviously, Don Pedro knew what was happening at his home while he was gone. The robbers were sobbing and expressed their anxiety to Don Pedro, saying, "why did you not come back sooner?" That's how my grandmother ended her Don Pedro story.

I learned that Don Pedro did not display or use his powers to directly punish the robbers despite his extraordinary abilities. He could have, but Don Pedro was also following the customary human-made rules created by the collective. This means humanity will have to do the work.

Don Pedro also showed up as an ordinary human being with a policeman by his side. He handed the robbers to the police and expected them to perform their task to protect society, to keep the peace and order. Don Pedro sees the importance of established human structure, to have it, work in service for the people. When other members of the community go out of alignment, they should be paying their dues. Karma has got its ways to collect its dues in the 3D realm to bring about the payback time is an aspect of this reality. Every human being is a part of the collective, and each one has a vote on how we are to live on earth. Everything on earth can shift and change as we choose to shift and change. "We create the rules in society whether we know it or not, or like it or not because we are made to be co-creators." And this is my golden realization after hearing Don Pedro's story from my Lola Senyang.

Don Pedro is our family guide. My daughter Radhaa and I had always invited Don Pedro to our family healing circle, bringing healing light into our family tree. No one knows how much healing we have done for everyone. That part, we are more than happy to do whether anyone realizes it or not. It's because we consider it as our sacred duty, which we were born to perform.

In the many times when Don Pedro appeared to us, it started as a knock. He knocks on a wall, on a refrigerator, or he knocks on a ceiling and lets us know of his presence with us. But he had never knocked on my front door like this one.

In the past, when Don Pedro knocked, Radhaa intuitively and quickly picked it up that Don Pedro has a very important message. We enjoyed connecting with Don Pedro through channeling or psychic conversations. In this way, it filled us with his wisdom, love, guidance and helped raise our frequency.

In the last several years, Radhaa and I have been going through many personal shifts and upgrades. The changes that have been happening to each of us were so intense, dramatic, life-changing, and considered transformative.

Moving from the West Coast to the East Coast was taxing to our bodies and our minds. Our relationship with our partners and other people shifted as well. Relocating disrupted our healing space and affected our relationship, especially with Don Pedro.

Several years ago, Radhaa and I created an amazing healing sanctuary at Hollywood Hills, California. A very special place where we daily channeled Don Pedro. Our healing space was a spiritual-magical vortex, a very unusual place for Los Angeles. It was nestled in a valley-like setting that felt like it was in the belly of the earth, yet to get there, one has to get up to the top of the hill. It was cocooned with forest trees, large exotic bird of paradise plants, and giant ferns. The patio is so large and expansive, it looked over the City of Angels, and we view the star-lights at night with delight.

Many mystical experiences came out of that space. It holds us near and dear to the spirit world. The few years we lived there seemed like many lifetimes. I have encountered dwarf beings, dead people who appeared to me, asking healing who were trapped on the 3D earth, who needed help to move forward into the afterlife.

Sorcerer-like beings came, and we experienced their presence. It was also common for some of them to practice black magic on others, which they tried on us, but failed. The light source of this universe always protected us. There were also our clients, unique people coming for healing, drawn to our sacred space. To top it with delight, our regular sessions with Don Pedro were powerful and out of this world. But sadly, that had diminished to almost nothing after we moved out of this vortex.

When the knock came to North Carolina, I realized that Don Pedro was calling me back. I had been in a total disconnect from him, and I knew he was not pleased with this. Don Pedro had been patiently waiting until enough is enough. That was when he appeared with his powerful knocks! Don Pedro wanted to re-awaken me back to the essential mission of my life - work with his Lemurian spirit, so I reconnected intentionally again with him.

Visions flooded my mind. I thought of the changing times we were in right now compared to our Hollywood sanctuary. It was a time when Radhaa and I were taking in so many clients, back-to-back, daily.

Don Pedro is telling me that more people need our support now more than ever, telling me to get out of my mindset of over-thinking things out. He is encouraging me to put more effort into making choices that will benefit more people, such as in my writing, a form of practical-intelligent-spiritual service to humanity. I know Don Pedro and my guides want me to expand my ability to be creative, be in service, enjoy my sacred work on earth and evolve even faster at this time. Don Pedro also told me that 2019 and beyond are years of many changes. It will take human willpower to run the new engine that will propel humanity to its next height. That is work, he says. But for those who can intentionally put their hearts and minds into this time, manifestation awaits.

It was clear that Don Pedro wanted me to mold my creation until results are achieved. I heard him. His knocking at my door is an urgent reminder for me not to get too far into the mundane realm. Instead, cultivate an even deeper spiritual realm in my life. He also told me that it's time to dream the real dream, where anything is possible, where barriers no longer exist between dimensions. It is where Don Pedro exists, with no barriers between dimensions. Free. Sovereign. Liberated.

ABOUT THE AUTHOR

Maya The Shaman

Maya Verzonilla, AKA Maya The Shaman, is a Shaman-Healer and multi-media artist from a family of Shaman-Healers. She was born in Los Banos, Laguna, in Maharlika (the Philippines), once a part of a large ancient Pacific continent — known as Lemuria or Mu. Shamans, healers, mystics, and sacred land keepers come from this place. "Descendants of Lemuria" is a memoir book that Maya is currently writing, expected to be published by 2022.

Maya followed the footsteps of her ancestral Lemurian lineage and created her original healing modality called "Lemurian Code Healing."

Having had a longstanding practice in Hollywood Hills, California, Maya served her clients and the greater Los Angeles area for over a decade. Moving to the Appalachian mountain of North Carolina after serving Los Angeles, Maya now offers long-distance healing to her clients.

Maya's discovery of her healing abilities started with clients from her store, Iris Blossom, in Ashland, Oregon, as a wearable art clothing and jewelry designer over two decades ago in the '90s. Her clients told her that it is because of her creations - and her - that they come back yearly. Such close relationships with devoted clients opened up many unexpected emotional connections. Sobbing women would walk into her store, telling her all types of unfortunate stories and disasters from their personal lives. Maya sincerely listened and supported their healing needs and, after they unloaded their stories, walked out smiling, relieved (also taking her artful creations). Being a healer was second nature to Maya.

She is also the mother of two amazingly creative children, Radhaa and Zen.

"Always an Artist, Healing is now her Art."
Maya is a Creative Writer Coach, Author, Shaman Healer of Original Modality "Lemurian Code Healing" & "Infinite Cosmic Records."

———

You can reach Maya at: 310-933-2568 by text
Website: www.MayaTheShaman.com

～

3

INCANTATIONS
PAST, PRESENT AND FUTURE HEALING

By LYN PACIFICAR

I am Katuuran* Lyn Pacificar, a Bisayan Albularyo of Waray and Ilonggo lineage, a descendant of Katuuran Apong Mansanat, born and living on Tongva territory in East Hollywood. It is with ancestral permission that I share the messages of my journey with you so that you may know what has happened in the past and what is to come. These incantations are channeled from the journey during the arrival of the solar flares, forty hours of fasting, the beginning of my moon blood time, with a waning moon in Capricorn.

"The Native Spirits of this land are my ancestors. I hear the deep sound of drums in my blood. Their ceremonial cries around the fires, calling forth their animal totems. Thousands of years ago, they arrived—crossing into unknown territories of treacherous topographies, led by chief and shaman. Tribes intermingling, creating new rituals and shifting the tides of time. Through their dreams, they traveled and saw me—knowing they would be

remembered and honored one day. Remnants of symbols, incantations, stories, and lost languages.

The ancestors were lied to and betrayed. Their love, kindness, and compassion crushed, like bones after cremation. The tongues of the women were removed, so they could not speak the truth. Their long hair was cut and used for power and pleasure by the ones who claimed Enlightenment. Children were made as slaves, and their men castrated or killed. Thrown into a river, washing away the memories of their existence. The land covered with trees, pregnant with gold, sacred property—impregnated with the seeds of fear, anger, pain, loss.

Centuries later, I reach up to the skies and catch their ashes enfolded in my hands. I hold it against my chest. Welcome home back to my heart—a proper burial in my being. Stronger than I ever was before. I carry your spirits to sing your songs; to perform your rituals; to bring forth the lands you once roamed upon. You will stand whole once again. I will give good medicine to all your descendants. I will wipe the tears, blood, and bruises away to remember you with my lips speaking the incantations, restoring the land—your people.

Heal the land. Healing creates connections between this realm and the realm of Spirit, gathering the ancestors to support the work from the other side.

The Dark One does not belong here and is no longer needed. The entities that have been present and caused harm are not allowed to do so anymore. The time is now to go and do the work for the next coming changes. Great earth changes and challenges to humanity. Healing is necessary and not an option. Believing is not a luxury. The Spirit realm is in preparation. Do what you must do to continue to succeed and make life as sustainable as you can. Don't hold onto things, and don't hold your breath. Nothing will harm you, nor your family. You are safe to do your work. The information you need and the resources you seek will all be provided for you in exchange for your services to humanity and our Earth planet. Others are waiting for your signal and the word to be sent through your ancestors. The realms communicate on different wavelengths & channels. Specific & clear. They need to be opened. Some are closed and have not been opened in over eons since the time of your great ancestors when the ritual was the place to speak to us. Angels. Angelic & Cosmic Beings. Receive this energy. Receive this wisdom. Truth is not always in the light. Truth is also in the dark."

When I wrote all of this down into my journal, I was in a trance. I was furiously transcribing thoughts that were being channeled through my hands and onto paper. I received clear downloads of information as I sat on the floor of my healing room, which once belonged to my father when he was alive. I was so exhausted after being overcome with all these messages, having no food for two days, and surviving off the water. My menstrual cycle began, and I was at my most powerful and sensitive time of the month for doing intense magical work—simultaneous cleansing and clearing energies within my body and Spirit! Thankfully, my husband, Gilbert, was able to accompany me with drumming to journey into the Spirit realm.

My *ninuno* (ancestors) shared their stories with me. It was essential to them that I knew where I come from. It mattered that I was aware of my bloodlines and my magic.

These roots, deep and robust, cannot be challenged. Conscious of what happened to my more recent ancestors, it's hard to swallow the fact that a mission to save the souls of "savages" (a word they used during the time of Christianization in the Philippines) that conquered lands in the name of Church and sovereignty; a proclamation that caused the genocide of several indigenous cultures. Much needed ancient healing practices for the Motherland await.

Acknowledging that these atrocities happened without reparations or compensation from the institution that usurped ancestral lands and murdered its children as part of my decolonization* and coming into my power as a Katu-uran. These traumas were inherited, written into some of my DNA. Not all my ninuno were convinced of the new religion as being in alignment with their belief systems. I began to heal the wounds with my birth, have brought the truth to the lies, restored trust to the betrayals, mended broken hearts, and connected dreams to my lineage. I AM an ancestor, returning to teach new rituals to the priestess and the people, to bring wholeness and wellness as a unified global community.

The Ancient Ones lived in harmony with the land. Everything had a spirit, and these spirits were interconnected with their own. It was understood that these were essential relationships to maintain the health and well-being of the community. Weaving energies with the Spirits of the land was an everyday practice. Plants, animals, rocks, rivers, oceans were acknowledged and appeased through offerings and prayer. Time was according to the sun, moon, and celestial bodies. These are no longer prevalent practices in our modern world. Instead, a culture of instant gratification and technological advancements exists, leading to the ravenous appetites of humans for faster and more advanced machinery—the next big thing to entertain ourselves with.

In my journey through the underworld, I heard, "The connection between Mother Earth and humans become further damaged and will ultimately be severed." Being cognizant and caring for our relationships with people and the environment is crucial to saving the future for all generations. Open your eyes, mind, heart, and soul to the land you dwell on. Create a container of space for you to center and listen to it through the trees, the sounds of the birds, the mountains, and your surroundings.

"What does the land need? What options can you think of to create a lifestyle of living in balance with Mother Earth? Where can you be of service to the Spirits of the land to bring back harmony and healing?"

At the core of this incantation contains the urgency to heal Mother Earth to heal our past, present, and future. This is a call to action for all light and shadow workers. The Ancient Ones encourage us to follow our hearts, live life to the fullest potential, stop wasting time, and get to it. If you are reading this now, you have been through much darkness. In that crepuscule of your awakening, you gained strength and the maps to navigate through all dimensions to assist in the Great Reclamation—a time in which a new Earth will be created. The angelic beings are with you to protect and support you in living your purpose. May we move together with the compassion, courage, peace, integrity, and love to restore our world.

*Katuuran: I received this designation through the journey delivered directly from my ancestors. A Katuuran is a person who obtains direction and immediately follows the protocol ritual to access the truth in healing and giving guidance. Baylan was the other name, and hence the custom of calling the said priestesses baylana...not all were equally esteemed (referencing to those who do not follow strict protocols). Katuuran, which means 'they who were more reliable and more credible; hence, people had greater recourse to them.' -Francisco Alcina, History of the Bisayan People in the Philippine Islands, 1668, p. 257.

*Decolonization, which sets out to change the order of the world, is, obviously, a program of complete disorder. But it cannot come as a result of magical practices, nor of a natural shock, nor *of a friendly understanding. Decolonization, as we know, is a historical process: that is to say, it cannot be understood, it cannot become intelligible nor clear to itself except in the exact measure that we can discern the movements which give it historical form and content.*

-Franz Fanon, The Wretched of the Earth, 1963, p. 36

ABOUT THE AUTHOR

Lyn Pacificar

Katuuran Lyn Pacificar is of Ilongga and Waray lineage descended from Katuuran Apong Mansanat, daughter of a manghihilot Filipino Martial Arts Master. She receives ancestral direction and follows protocoled ritual to access the truth in healing and delivers its guidance by using a combination of modalities including prayers, hilot (a traditional form of manual energetic therapy), diagnostic readings, and spirit communication and serves as a mouthpiece of her *ninuno* (ancestors) to help people access their own medicine and powers of self-healing. Also, she maintains her connection to ancestral lands and manages farms on the islands of Dinagat, Panay, and Mindanao.

Katuuran Lyn Pacificar is the founder/creatrix/CEO of Herbalaria, a company that creates culturally rooted, spiritual, indigenous medicine into contemporized all-natural and organic wellness products. Her passion for the community has led her to organize group healing rituals, host traditional tattooing in her home, facilitate workshops on traditional plant and energy medicine, and volunteer for various non-profits and cultural causes. She is a certified Reiki Master of Usui Holy Fire Reiki Lineage and currently lives on Tongva land in East Hollywood, California, with her family.

Websites: www.herbalaria.com
And www.lynpacificar.com
Contact: info@herbalaria.com

∾

4

STRANGER THAN FICTION
DREAMING OF OTHER WORLDS

By SUSAN HASSEN

I lead an unconventional life. When I wake up in the morning and go to work, I walk into the Quantum Field, a major change from where I was headed, a corporate career in the field of law. But life is funny that way.

I have spent the last five years of my life working as a Quantum Energy Healer, specifically practicing Quantum Sphere Healing, where I access the Quantum Field to shift the patterning underlying emotional and physical traumas.

Today I work in the higher dimensions, but looking back at my life, it seems so obvious that I would one day awaken to my Starseed roots. I remember the feelings of not belonging in my youth, the angst, the waves of intense emotions, the dreaming of other worlds, and the obsession with all things "outer space." What I didn't know when I was experiencing these things is that they were all clues. They were all leading me to what I've known all along that my true nature is Oneness and that I come from the 'stars - that' my life here is not meant to be ordinary, that love and compassion are the real pillars of my being, and that I am always expanding and growing- and that means to discover the truth about this reality: that we are the Universe. There was still an unexplained pull to the stars within me. There was always existential angst I could not grasp in childhood. Why was I here? Why is anyone here? What even is God? What is the point of it all? My escape from this boredom and ennui was outer space. I knew I didn't belong on Earth, and I knew I needed to go home. Why did I always feel like "I am the only one" in anything that I ever felt and did?

Becoming a "truther" was what ultimately led to my spiritual awakening. I had always questioned political agendas in the back of my mind as I was furthering my education. When I was in law school, I began to pay more attention to how society functioned as a whole, and I saw injustice everywhere. During the "Occupy Wall Street" movement, I decided I couldn't sit back and be part of a world that promoted greed and capitalism. I started to see that I was connected to everyone's struggle, that I was the ninety-nine percent. This was also when I discovered Monsanto and the dangers of GMOs. And so, I began to attend protests and develop my activism.

My voice for truth and freedom started to emerge, but the spiritual aspect was missing. My activism was fueled by anger at the system. I only knew how to "fight the power" and create change by way of protest. I still needed to learn how to be the change. As I was getting ready to graduate from law school, I began to have a series of spiritual awakenings. I truly awaken from the dream. I was beginning to see energies and experience intense visitations from extraterrestrials. All the pieces came together. I realized that we indeed lived in a matrix created by people and beings, keeping us in a state of fear, panic, and sleep. The world felt very dark and hopeless. I felt trapped, and I didn't know a way out. I didn't think there was a way out, and I certainly didn't think I had any power or say in the matter.

I moved along my journey, learning everything I could about dark entities, extraterrestrials, and the forces that keep the Matrix in play. It was the darkest point in my journey of awakening. I was in constant hyper-vigilance, looking out for psychic attacks from entities and dark forces as I used my voice and social media platforms at the time to spread awareness. I didn't know there was a light at the end of the tunnel, and I didn't realize that I was the light guiding me through the darkness. Was this it? Do you just learn about all the conspiracy theories and horrible truths about this reality until you die? Do you ever make it out of the Matrix? The stress of my reality at the time, paired with my loss of interest in a legal career, took its toll on my health. I developed challenging health issues that Western medicine could not correctly heal. It was the highest blessing I could ever ask for because it inspired me to seek out the help of a Shaman.

Up until this point, my reality was as bleak as it could get. In my eyes, the collective was asleep, and dark forces were feeding off our consciousness.

We were batteries for the Matrix. Something in me started to crack. I needed Spirit. I needed a connection to the Universe as I had when I was a child. Upon awakening, I had deprogrammed myself from mainstream religion, and it stripped me of most of my spiritual beliefs, but what remained was the energy of truth. I realized that since I was a child, I was always searching for the highest truth, and this remains my ultimate guiding light. I am my Source. I knew I had an inner light, and I wanted to feel it again. I began studying shamanism, Sufism, Eastern Religions of the world, philosophy, and read sources of channeled information and teaching from various spiritual leaders and gurus. I needed to know everything. I needed to find a way out.

As my health concerns grew, the Universe connected me to a Shaman. She performed remote shamanic healings on me and helped me successfully overcome my health issues. She guided me through shadow work, inner child work, emotional healing, but most importantly, she introduced me to the concept of the Higher Self. This was the moment I spiritually awakened. All my life finally led me to what I have always been seeking my beloved Higher Self. I was finally reintroduced to my ancient self, my unlimited power, my ultimate guide, and the part of me unrestricted and unbound by form. Life began to make sense finally. I was not alone and abandoned, like how I felt when I had awakened to a dark and dreary Matrix. I had the ultimate "spirit guide" on my side, and I could access it through myself!

Soon after, my Shaman invited me to take her workshop on a new healing modality she created called Quantum Sphere Healing. I had no prior healing experience, but something told me I should go for it. When the workshop began, the first thing I did was a journey to the Fifth Dimension and met my Higher Self - face to face. It was like a homecoming. It was emotional, uplifting, and life-changing. I finally felt like the spiritual part of my life I had been chasing had also been chasing me, and we finally met with nowhere to run but into each other's arms. With the guidance of my Higher Self, I instantly excelled at my workshop. Quantum Sphere Healing fits like a glove. It was destiny - it was the career path I had always dreamed of and one that I had no idea I was preparing for my entire life. I jumped right in and never looked back.

My Starseed journey has taught me that to change the

world, the first place I had to start was in myself. That if I heal myself, I can help improve the world because we are all connected. It was not about protesting the man and fighting the good fight out on the streets. It was about healing the trauma and emotions that made me want to fight for the world. It has taught me that I had not genuinely awakened until I had awakened to Oneness and that I am still awakening every day.

It has taught me that my mission here was never to fit in but just to be here and seed my unique energy signature and gifts into the Earth so that I can assist in the collective's awakening. My mission is to bring more light, and I do this by serving others through my healing practice while also honoring my human experience. Our humanity allows us to empathize with others, but our cosmic roots remind us that there are no others - that we are truly the one light, the one Source, the one God. My journey also confirmed to my eight-year-old self that aliens indeed exist; I just never expected I would be one of them. But that's how Starseed awakenings go: we remember, and we forget. We do it repeatedly until the truth is stranger than fiction, but it just feels right, and listening to what feels right and true for ourselves is what we're all here to do until we become who we truly are, and the time comes for us to go back home.

Starseed Sayings:

"If we are serious about dreaming our awakening into being and creating a peaceful, loving earth in which the heart, spirit and soul are the only true leaders, we must continue to keep our focus on thoughts of unity and all that truly brings us together."
— **Diane Hall**

ABOUT THE AUTHOR

Susan Hassen

Susan Hassen is a Quantum Sphere Healer, holistic practitioner, emotional counselor, author, activist, and Juris Doctor. She runs the blog CosmicArcheress.com where she uses her background in higher dimensional healing, emotional body, and energy bodywork to assist humanity in our spiritual evolution. Susan lives in Los Angeles, California, where she teaches workshops and gives talks promoting self-love, healing, and empowerment to spread consciousness and inspire others to do the same. Susan is currently expanding her healing practice and introducing unconventional and out of this world, healing modalities to help others overcome both their physical and emotional obstacles.

To book a Quantum Sphere Healing session with Susan visit her website quantumspherehealer.com. To read her published works and original content, visit her blog cosmicarcheress.com, and to keep up with her on Instagram follow @quantumspherehealer.

5

UNCONSCIOUS TO SUPERCONSCIOUS

By STASIA BLISS

On the floor eating my karma! I had an awakening from my future self again.

I slammed my fists into the floor of my mother's house, crying. I had run home after failing with my second child's father. "Why is this happening to me again?" I screamed through snot and tears.

I'd wished so much for my mother's gentle hand to support my back, to give me the motherly love, and I ached for. Couldn't she just cry with me? Let me feel her loving me? Instead, her words cut sharply through my sobs. Where I wanted her to be a soft place to land my shaken heart, she instead showed me words sharper than the Balinese Kriss I carry today to remind me who I am.

I knew she meant well. My four sisters, my brother, and I were raised as the oddball, strict Mormon family in the tiny town of Boring, Oregon. I followed all the rules and did everything I was supposed to, curious as I was. What resonated with my soul most, however, was playing with the fairies in our giant yard, being mischievous with the neighbor boys, and long talks about quantum physics and multiple realities with my father.

In my daddy's mind, he was musing just for fun, all about the possibilities in the universe. Still, to me, he was not just crafting whimsical stories. For me, those long nights of outrageous mind-bending talks were slowly helping me decode deep remembrances within.

I remember when it first happened. It was the same crumbling I was feeling on the floor. It was like mirrors opened on both sides, and eternity stretched eerily out in both directions. I suddenly saw myself, in the life I had created, forever. I had done it. I had followed all the rules and repressed my sexual urges through boyfriend after boyfriend. Passed on the drugs and alcohol, didn't smoke the cigarette, didn't get fingered, and didn't party. I married the guy in a temple-marriage way and ended up in this religiously healthy relationship where sex felt to be bartered as love. And it sucked. Babies would no doubt soon come, and I suddenly wondered what the hell I just sign up for? I had looked forward to my whole life for this, and now what? Just sustain it like we have been practicing. *Homemaking, Kids, Choir, Church, Temple, Repeat?* I could not. The thought of it repelled me. If I was going to sustain something for the time and all eternity, was I really sure this was all there was?

Everything in me was searching for the exit point - even though my conscious mind had no clue what to do. The betrayal of my temple marriage in the most sinful way possible was the only way the constructs of my early upbringing could formulate to execute to access a loophole out. My husband fell to the floor, shaking and sobbing when he learned I would leave him. I remember we called an ambulance because it looked like he was having a seizure. I was not sure if I should feel responsible in some way. When the Bishop told me God was unhappy with me for the choices, I just knew I was done. Deep inside, I knew that whatever this God was, I knew I was FULLY LOVED no matter what - and what was most important was the way I felt about myself inside.

My mother's words again rang out, though they seemed to curse me when she learned I would divorce my husband.

"You are going to end up an old maid like your Aunt Joyce."

I would spend the next 20 years of my life wading through my own belief in curses and every program and judgment set up for me in my early training.

Man after man would enter and leave my life. My first marriage lasted two years, and my second, only five months. The longest relationship I had was with Nathan- the man I had an affair with. It also eventually contained several relationships within it - including my only relation- ship with a woman and our stretch into polyamory. That beautiful man was the catalyst for so much inner transfor- mation. Eight years of our very bumpy and all-encom- passing relationship ended with the event that our union could not contain.

Dreams predicted what would happen, though I could not have imagined how. A spacecraft had taken me one night and told me that I would have a Star-child from another planet - I felt them tell me he would be unique. I had agreed. I remember my father trying to dissuade me, but maybe he only represented my old limiting beliefs.

Outside of an Ayahuasca ceremony in Central Oregon, I stared up into the moonless night. The stars were as bright as I had remembered them in the Himalayas. They felt as though they were right over my head and talking to me. One of them seemed to jump right into my womb, and at that moment, I knew.

My sweet loving Nathan, my Nath yogi - he must have hated that the star-child coming through me after our eight years together was using his guru's DNA, not his. He knew I had a dream which foretold it. He hated himself for having agreed to abort my first pregnancy with him, so he could take me to see the world instead, which I love him for.

I love that I have seen as much of this world as I have. We experienced so much magic together.

That purifying force that was shattering my universe again on the floor beside my mother came through Nathan back then. I could see it, and there was no way for his mind to continue at its same viewpoint when he learned of the child in my womb - Heritage.

So many auspicious occurrences happened before that moment under the stars. After the initiations, ceremony after ceremony, blessing after blessing, teacher, guru, saint, master - all blessing me, giving me gifts, working on me was surreal.

No man could stay with me long through the many awakening initiations which would follow. One more, two more, ten more relationships later - stripped down even more - here I was feeling to be in the very same position I had seen those men in, on the floor, shattered, and I had another new child with me now.

My mother's words thundered as if from a future time-line - one where the empowered me lived. "You made this bed." She firmly stated in my direction, not phased a bit by my gestures of self-pity. As bitter as her words dropped on my soul and as cold as her seemingly friendless hand, she was right. And she was more than a best friend to me right then.

This beautiful six-month-old baby sat next to me - Karuna Ray. His dad had appeared to me as the biggest narcissist in the book. He belittled me and challenged all my earliest girl dreams to the core. He broke me, my heart, but also the fantasy I had of men and love - at least the one I was given growing up. He was my dance with the devil. He showed me everything I despised about myself. From his not showing up, I began to show up more for myself.

Every relationship began to reveal itself to me anew. My relationship with my inner being took on more life. An integration begins to occur as I filed back through all my relationships to find the purpose for them and the way love had shown up for me through them. My heart opened to a higher degree than ever. I was learning to love myself for all of it.

Today, when there is music - I dance, a drum - I drum, a guitar - I strum. I follow the signs because I believe life is talking to me all the time. I play silly with my kids. We take turns eating healthy and eating like shit. We sometimes scream at each other. We love to snuggle. I tell them who I see them be - little Masters in the flesh, here to Be their fullest, most awesome selves; however, they find they are here to do that.

And the loveliest transformation for me - I fell in love with a man, and I have decided I will keep going with it, no matter what we face, distant or apart. I choose him. I am choosing him repeatedly, which is just the choice to keep choosing myself at a deeper and more profound level and increasingly love myself. He forces me to spend time with myself. After all, he likes his time too - which I appreciate because he is so lovely. I could sit by him forever and do nothing else but enjoy his presence. But I have fallen in love with myself. Much needed time and opportunity to be a mom to the coolest kids on earth. And I love my man for being authentic with me and loving me for who I am, and showing me that I love myself a lot.

I admit, some concepts from Mormonism I choose to keep - like the idea of becoming Gods and Goddesses one day creating your universe - though, for me, these concepts are not to be realized after death and judgment day, but right NOW and in every moment.

ABOUT THE AUTHOR

Stasia Bliss

Stasia Bliss is a Unity-Consciousness Alchemical Visionary Writer, Embodiment Speaker, Kundalini Educator, and Empowerment Coach. Her presence anchors the Unity field and entrains others to a New Paradigm of Love and Higher Relationship. Having navigated her own Awakening Journey since 1997 and after spending years traveling throughout Asia and SE Asia, teaching yoga and meditation, modeling, mothering, studying, and experiencing life and relationship from a yogic perspective as well as navigating the deep inner realms through both entheogens and various disciplines, she admits she is excited to both witness and assists the world is going through this very profound process of mass Kundalini Awakening - as a collective.

Stasia is an Evolutionary Mental Health Coach and Multi-Dimensional Healer who assists individuals, couples, and groups in releasing defeating subconscious mind conditioning, clearing, and integrating ancestral karma and past-life memories, activating higher capacities in the DNA, shamelessly embracing intimacy, sensuality, and sexuality from a Tantric perspective, understanding how to masterfully work with Kundalini life-force energy, and tuning into the resonant field of Love.

As Tantric Dakini, Stasia holds a non-judgmental love space for others to tune into primordial awareness and receive validation, healing, attunement, and inspiration to remember who they are and why they are here.

With 10 published books and thousands of online articles, hundreds of videos and audio presentations, and meditations, Stasia Bliss is a powerful voice in empowering others to live a life of authenticity, personal truth, and divine embodiment. See Stasia's Online presence below:

Website: www.blissinthehouse.com
And through:
Facebook Public Profile
YouTube channel
Amazon Author page.
Basmati.com Soundcloud, Spreaker,
Instagram, Twitter, LinkedIn, & Pinterest

～

6

PARENTHOOD AS A SPIRITUAL JOURNEY

By JOSHUA HATHAWAY

Fathering my Starseed child has been my toughest spiritual practice, my most transformative rite of passage, and the most significant thing I've ever done.

Make no mistake! This journey of parenting has kicked my ass repeatedly and again. I have failed to live up to my own standards as a parent countless times along the way. I have had to grow up right alongside him. I have done many things I felt ashamed of, and I have apologized to my son innumerable times. Maybe I "could have" done better by him. At the end of the day, I feel proud of how I have shown up for him and grateful for the ways his mother has devoted herself to him.

My 17-year-old son, Skye, is the smartest person I know. He is a Junior in High School, carrying a 4.6 GPA, vying for valedictorian of his class against two of his best friends. He wears Stanford socks to school most days because he is devoted to getting admitted to the best University in the world on a full-ride scholarship to study Environmental Science and restore the planet.

It's actually kinda crazy.

You see, Skye was Un-Schooled for seven years between the ages of 7 and 14. No "math homework." No "core curriculum." He was seldom coerced into doing anything he didn't want to do (though he might tell it differently). Just countless hours of first listening to, and then reading, hundreds of books. Innumerable projects with Legos, cardboard, leather, digital media, and eventually, a forge (yes, the hammering was glowing steel into sharp objects kind). An unbroken series of stage performances, screenplays, short films, and short stories. A semi-religious commitment to spending a full day in the local landscape each week with trusted mentors—learning the names of the flowers and trees, how to construct a primitive shelter, track an animal through the woods and build a fire with nothing but a knife and some sticks.

Now he is one of the most considerate, honest, mature people I know.

Skye's a beautiful example of what is possible when we *trust our children* and commit ourselves—against all conventional wisdom and strong currents of mainstream society—to *discover who they are alongside them* instead of defining who they are for them. Our Starseeds do not need to be fixed or trained but are only given the proper conditions and nutrients for their gifts to grow and thrive.

For all our shortcomings as parents, Skye did receive the benefit of many conscious decisions from the time of his conception. It contributed to who he is today. I want to give a shortlist of those before going into the core of what all these strategies are based on:

Skye's mother took incredibly loving care of herself

while he was in the womb: nutritionally and spiritually. She never even let the midwife do an ultrasound to protect his developing energy body from the potentially harmful frequencies of the equipment. He was born at home without the use of any drugs, despite being a whopping 10 lbs and 3 oz when he finally slid out of her body after *2.5 hours of pushing*! The day he was born, Skye (and his mom) received an at-home Network Chiropractic Entrainment, and he has spent his whole Life getting regular Network care. We never even considered mutilating his little penis, so he remains unshorn. We refused all vaccinations for him in the face of insistent doctors at his 2-week checkup (I would not even let them put the thermometer in his butt–– "Um, that's a tender little one-way street, ma'am. His armpit will do just fine."). And, thanks to lots of alternative care and a medicine mama committed to herbs and tradi-tional remedies, he has only ever taken antibiotics ONCE in his 17 years! He never watched television or was exposed to screens until after he weaned off his mother's breast at 2.5 years old. And even then, we were VERY selective about the quality and amount of time he spent in front of a screen.

I want to emphasize here that we did all of this while receiving Medi-Cal and living in HUD-subsidized housing. We did our research. We found practitioners who were either willing and able to take our state coverage, prepared to work on partial trade or who could put us on adjusted or low-income payment plans. We did what we needed to do to make sure that Skye received the quality of care he deserved in our eyes.

We were young and idealistic. And we were fortunate to find a set of principles early on that would help us embody our belief in Skye's innate wholeness in clear and practical ways throughout the years to come: Nonviolent Communication, by Marshall Rosenberg, Ph.D.

After hearing a local teacher of NVC speaking on public radio, I went out and bought the book that would change my Life forever. The current edition is called "Compassionate Communication." Compassionate Communication tools have been central not only to my practice of relationships on all levels since then but to my career. I drank the Kool-Aid and committed to teaching people from all walks of Life, especially parents, about this incredible practice.

Rosenberg was able to distill a set of practices for communicating and listening antithetical to the kinds of subtle violence we do every day with our words, especially to children. By focusing on sharing our experience through describing our Observations instead of projections, Feelings instead of thoughts, and owning our universal human needs as the basis of our emotions, we can speak the truth without judgment by deeply respecting the sovereignty of other people and focusing on making Requests instead of demands. We cultivate Power-With relationships instead of power-over dynamics. And when we listen with empathy to the feelings and needs of others instead of reacting defensively to their words and actions, we create the possibility of deep connection and have a much harder time taking other people's shit personally.

Embodying these principles has become one of my central spiritual practices. Parenting a sovereign being with empathy—using as little threat and coercion as humanly possible—became the hardest and most important thing I have ever done.

No parent needs more reasons to be ashamed. If you are a parent who has regrets, please be *kind* and forgiving with yourself. None of us can go back and change what we did not know to do for our children in the past.

That said, it is NEVER too late to commit to learning and embodying these principles starting right now to create a whole new future for ourselves and our beloved Starseeds.

It's one thing to *believe* in a child's Original Innocence, and it's another thing to *live in the fire* of honoring that, day in and day out, when we have been conditioned to treat children as second-class citizens at best and property at worst. The path of conscious parenting requires us to come back to ourselves and our own values day in and day out.

A rite of passage I had to go through repeatedly as a father was letting go of making him in my image and likeness. And trust me, there were many days I did NOT like who my son *was* being!

But my conviction was to respect his developmental process, and ultimately his sovereignty. Instead of controlling his behavior (which would only sow the seeds of resentment and rebellion), I focused on instilling values in him that would long outlast my ability to punish. I would tell people that, "I would rather he be an asshole at eight years old than 18."

And it worked! (Phew!)

He's genuinely himself. He studies because he wants to. Now he climbs big walls in Yosemite and Red Rocks because he loves it (almost) as much as I do. Because we committed to doing OUR work to parent him nonviolently, Skye continues to discover who he is and what he is here to do to serve Life, with a lot less baggage than most of us.

And I don't have to pay for college!

Starseed Sayings:

"Empaths did not come into this world to be victims, we
came to be warriors. Be brave. Stay strong.
We need all hands on deck."
— **Anthon St. Maarten**

ABOUT THE AUTHOR

Joshua Hathaway

Joshua Hathaway, M.A. Holistic Clinical Psychology, is a Tongue Fu black belt and master of the Art of Connection. Through his private and organizational training in No Bullsh!t Communication, as well as coaching and consulting, Joshua is radically empowering people's success in the changing landscapes of modern love and leadership.

A 2005 graduate of the BayNVC North American Leadership Program, and a 2008 Master's graduate from JFK University, he brings almost two decades of research and practice in communication, psychology, and integral systems to the process of leveling up your emotional intelligence and communication skills.

Joshua is a dynamic coach and public speaker, able to gently and humorously dismantle people's Bullsh!t, deliver practical skill-building tools, and facilitate experiences that bring home the power and value of connection. With an artful combination of solid structure and intuitive navigation skills, he can meet every individual or large group he encounters right where they are and open doors into new territory.

Here they discover more honesty, the capacity to listen and communicate in healthier ways, greater acceptance and humor about inevitable relationship challenges, and increased confidence in creating meaningful connections across the relational landscape.

7

IN SEARCH FOR TRUTH

By CAPTAIN COSMIC

I believe in the supernatural realm, and it has sustained me through the darkest periods of my life.

My father was deported when I was ten years old. It marked a period of intense struggle for my nuclear family. My mother, brother, and I lost our home, and we lived out of our car for quite some time. All the trauma that my mother never dealt with started to surface. Years of abuse and unhealthy social conditioning turned her cold and bitter.

At the very young age of five, during my sleep, I had a profound experience. I witnessed a soul download. Remnants from other lives came into my physical memory. I vividly remembered having it flash right before me. I woke up unfamiliar with my surroundings. My family reminded me of my name, but it did not feel like mine. I continued to think about that "dream" for many years until realizing it was my first awakening.

The experience left me with the impression that there was something more to life. A feeling that magic was tucked away in the deepest dwellings of my being, waiting to be rediscovered. I constantly spoke to Spirit even if I received no response. I would often find a secretive, private spot and whisper, "please, God, show me something magical. You can trust me." Throwing in the occasional sass and eye-roll, "I know it's out there."

My faith in the supernatural was so real and overwhelming that it hurt me only to feel and witness the mundane realm. I often imagined God surprising me and showing me a secret doorway, a portal. Through it, I envisioned a new land where everything was serene and magical.

I toyed with my psychic abilities throughout my childhood. They stirred up within me as my mind wanted to explore the possibilities. It led me to find an abundance of evidence, many non-physical occurrences. I discovered I could predict events before they occurred. My dreams were prophetic or at least very revealing. I could hear other people's thoughts, and I was skilled in sculpting reality to my liking.

I was an ambitious little girl with a clear vision. As I grew older, I always sought to satisfy the wishes of my younger self.

Yet, I could sense underneath that there was anger that resided within me. My inner child was wounded from the abuse I had endured. As a young healer at heart, I began years of deprogramming generational pain.

My mother and I worked together towards redefining our love language. It was a radical transformation. We decided that we could no longer tolerate or allow the cycles of abuse to continue to be passed down in our family lineage. I thought of my future children and the many children who would follow. Unknowingly, my heart was being guided by the star children.

Our relationship with children needs to be mutual. We can learn a lot from them.

I routinely go out into nature and reconnect with the sense of freedom that children so effortlessly enjoy. In my youth, I tried to act older, and then when I got older, I saw from the lens of a curious child. Suddenly I felt much younger than I have ever felt. What a paradox!

So dear Beloveds, the ambition of the star children is similar to that of an inner child's. The two are cut from the same cloth, and both encourage silencing the logical mind to rediscover our true free-spirited nature. Loving adults are guided to give children a platform to voice their feelings. Much wisdom will be earned from this. Children will reveal that the make-believe is not a total fantasy—we make what we believe.

Children remind us of our ability to be bare. They teach us how to be raw and vulnerable with our Spirit and our bodies. Their basic needs are simple. Born with no initial concept of time, infants only honor their needs in the now-moment. They do not worry about what the future holds. They cry out when they need help, NOW.

Just like animals, provided with the proper environment, they are born with everything they need. A beautiful and rich life is possible with enough food, water, and shelter. A gazelle does not require the luxuries of a modern man to thrive. I say "the proper environment" because we know many improper environments exist. The greatest threat to children might be humans themselves, and it is not the luxuries that keep them safe. Even a finely secured mansion could not guarantee a child is free from abuse from within it.

Starseeds are being born on our planet right now. They arrive with a strong sense of purpose and cosmic awareness. Their souls are trained before being birthed. But the transition in entering this dense realm is abrupt and strenuous. If a child's psychic abilities are not actively engaged and encouraged, any extrasensory gifts are quickly forgotten.

I speak on behalf of the star children as an ambassador. They come to me and tug at my sleeve. They seek me out because of my secure connection with my inner child. Perhaps this is why many children today struggle with the feeling of being out of place.

I bring you a message from the Star Children presently on this planet and in the realms beyond. The children wish to express their unwavering love and compassion for the people of this Earth. Their hearts beat small but steadfast for their co-inhabitants: animals, plants, and the tiniest of insects. Children can feel compassion for the rocks, boulders, and natural structures of the world. Their energy runs rampant throughout all of existence. They wish to reawaken the child-like Spirit that lies dormant in many of us. They seek to watch and guide us with laughs along the way.

I predict that the children born many generations from now will have eyes as big as their hearts. Their heads will develop to be larger, as will the adults, to accommodate all they know. Even today, children are born with a great sense of understanding before it is conditioned to be suppressed. Even on an instinctual level, infants and children contain the toolkit to sustaining life on this planet. Like a newborn animal with its mother, they will naturally and intuitively learn how to walk, talk, and eat.

My 'I am' now has evolved to 'We are.' My story is no longer out of the ordinary as it once might have been. Many are starting to reawaken and remember their own experiences of the extraordinary. Taking a moment to revisit childhood memories will reveal that they were not minor events after all. There is a tremendous amount of magic in the world. I always pause to admire the countless miracles I have witnessed. The starships that have shown up before me to blink, wave, twist, and turn. They are as significant to me as the love I have learned and the forgiveness I have unearthed.

The nature of children is pure. Go outside and play. Have fun. Laugh for the sake of it. Tell others how you feel, similar to a child who compliments your every piece of clothing. Look others in their eyes and make a connection. Ask them if they want to be friends. Remember, there is not always physical evidence for what you perceive. Trust that what you feel is real. Not everything will have a logical explanation because some things are meant to be explored. Use your discernment and figure out what is right for you to develop your own ideas, not based on what others tell you to believe in. Open yourself to what the Unseen is communicating to you through a type of extrasensory feeling.

The glowing star child that lives within you longs to greet you once again. Feel them in your heart space now. If you feel you have heard these messages before, it is because you have. The children sing it like one of their songs. These messages have circulated for millennia in a constant effort to trigger remembrance.

We forget that we are "members" of the collective of "All That Is." In our embodiment, we are the body members of Spirit. That includes the children and the equally important role they play.

Namaste

Starseed Sayings:

"As the New Earth approaches, our way of thinking is being challenged more and more. The Veil is thinning and lifting as our consciousness expands. This is a requirement for entering the new dimension with the raising of our vibrations and frequencies. The old paradigms and archaic belief systems must fall to the wayside to make room for the new."

— Dolores Cannon

ABOUT THE AUTHOR

Captain Cosmic

Captain Cosmic is an intuitive Theta Healer, Ascension Guide, and Psychic based in Albuquerque, New Mexico. After having a profound close-up physical experience with an extraterrestrial being in 2015, Captain has dedicated her life to working as a First Contact Specialist, preparing others for total disclosure. Captain works closely with the energies of the cosmos to provide clarity, healing, and relief to others on the awakening path while simultaneously helping to raise the vibration of all the places she encounters.

Captain often refers to herself as a "Cosmic Witch." She incorporates her cosmic awareness with a blend of traditional and modern forms of brujería. Captain studied at the local *Starlight School of Magic and Shamanism* and also holds training in Reiki, Theta Healing™, Curanderismo, and several forms of divination such as tarot and scrying.

In 2016, Captain was taught the art of reading Turkish coffee cups and has specialized in it ever since. Captain operates her own traveling metaphysical business, *The Cosmic Healing Shop*, brings healing tools to public spaces making them accessible, and travels to various cities and events.

Captain attained a Bachelor of Media Arts degree from the University of New Mexico and has integrated her love of digital arts with her passion for spirituality fit for the modern-day.

Captain works to make spiritual information more available using social media platforms to unite light-workers all over the world, marking the era of Web Witches and Internet-Mystics. Find Captain Cosmic on these platforms for ascension energy updates, ET talks, intuitive tarot readings, creative cosmic expression, and much more.

Instagram & Twitter: @cosmicaptain_
Youtube: Captain Cosmic @cosmicaptain_
Facebook.com/cosmicaptain
Email: cosmicaptain@gmail.com
Shop: @thecosmichealingshop

༄

8

COSMIC WAKE-UP CALL

By MICHELLE KEARNEY LOPEZ

One fateful night just after the Christmas holiday in 2005, I went to bed. I had resolved to do better than I had previously. I wanted to be a more committed wife and mother. I felt happy after celebrating Christmas with the family, and it gave me the resolve to commit more to my life.

That night, I woke up in a state of sleep paralysis.

I was completely lucid and aware of what was going on around me, and I was completely immobile. I could see dark beings, and I was frightened. Then suddenly, I felt my etheric body being ripped out of my physical body via the solar plexus. It was the most terrifying experience. I remember the next thing waking up, laying there feeling like I had the worst fever of my life.

I felt like I was on fire! My upper chakras were active, and I felt psychically lit up!

My life from that moment on would never be the same. I became acutely aware of another dimension that I only thought of as a metaphor. In hindsight, something miraculous was happening. I was being purified. However, at that time, I did not see it that way. My religious upbringing taught me to fear such things. I experienced many physical sensations that were quite dramatic. I often felt the presence of spirits and would see shadow beings around me.

Going to sleep each night became a challenge since the experiences continued during my dream time. I instinctively went to bed at night, covering my third eye with my hand.

I felt a tremendous amount of pressure on my crown chakra and brow chakra. It was extremely uncomfortable and made it very difficult to focus as I went about my daily activities. I was at a loss. What could these sensations be? I felt as if I were losing it. I sought out help. Was I possessed? Was I abducted? Was it a psychic attack? Did I need a priest? I went to see one and found a Catholic nun instead. She was quite knowledgeable in metaphysics and did not seem very surprised to hear about what I was going through. She instructed me to go home and take a salt bath and do a clearing at my home. So, I did just that.

Then there were the rays of light.

I began to experience this phenomenon of rays of light opening above my head. I would be going about my daily business, taking out the trash, or helping my children with their homework when the light ray would start raining down on my crown. It would happen hundreds of times a day and would continue for years. It felt as if hundreds of little sprinkles were falling on my head. It was quite intense, and now I understand these rays to be the seven rays of light that we all experience but are unaware of.

The chakra at the back of my crown felt as if it had a flame burning from it for many months. The best way to describe it is it was very much like a smokestack, and I was burning off lifetimes of karma.

After doing much research, I learned about the phenomenon of kundalini awakening. Initially, it was quite confusing because the description of the kundalini awakening was based on an Eastern interpretation. There was very little information on kundalini awakening from a Western perspective at that time. I equated it with the "holy spirit" because that is what it felt like to me.

My experience with it did not fit the classic description of kundalini awakening since mine was a top-down phenomenon. It was more of kundalini activation. In any case, the kundalini fire continued to move through me. I fiercely resisted the process, which made it very difficult. I remember thinking, "I would not wish this on my worst enemy!" My dreams were bizarre, and I had many visitations from unwanted spirits. My skin crawled and itched, and I felt like I was on fire. This persisted for many months.

After a time, I sought out psychiatric treatment for the anxiety I was experiencing, and my life went back to normal. I was not into holistic health like I am now and resorted to anxiety meds to help me get back on track. I felt good again, although you could say I went back to sleep to a certain degree. My perception of the light rays continued for a few years. I had to continue my life as a wife and mother and be strong for my children.

My children were in the center of my world, and I needed to feel normal again. These are what I call the "Disneyland years." There were trips to Disneyland filled with family bonding, joy, laughter, and the wonderment of childhood. It was a precious time in my life.

Fast forward to 2012. I felt an upliftment and felt compelled to move beyond the confines of religion.

I remember having thoughts to myself. "How am I going to come out of the closet?" I knew I could not continue to go through the expansion I was experiencing and stay in religion. The religion of my youth gave me peace for some time; however, religion is belief. It is not experience. In other words, the map is not the territory, and when you start walking in the territory of spirit, you begin, let go of the map because it becomes irrelevant at that point. I was in the territory. The yearnings of my soul and the desire for truth far outweighed any of the Earthly paradigms that I was programmed to believe.

Later, in March of 2012, as I lay in a morning twilight sleep, I heard what I believe to be a clarion call. It said, *"You have been chosen as transformers of the planet...change mindsets and thinking."* I literally sat up in bed and said to myself, "What...was...that?" It was so clear and so profound, and I knew the message was not just for me. The experiences continued, and I was having another awakening. I saw sparkles, flickers, and pins of light. The activity in my crown chakra began increasing once again, and I knew I had to find out more. I was being called.

Since that time, I have endured the most challenge. Little did I know at the beginning of 2012 that I would experience more enormous difficulties than those I have spoken of here. I went through a difficult divorce at the end of 2012, custody issues, and financial hardships.

I spent a week in psychiatric care and was labeled "crazy" by some.

I knew I was not crazy but could not explain what I now know to be alien implants as the cause of emotional distress and hallucinations. Who would have believed it? The two months I spent in outpatient therapy gave me a look at a part of life. I never thought I would see. Now, I could no longer see my children without supervised visits. While it looked like my third-dimensional world was falling apart, so was my internal world on a mental, emotional, and spiritual level.

I could relate it to what happens to a caterpillar when the caterpillar stops its previous life experience, cocoons itself, and becomes a gelatinous soup of imaginal cells. It can be likened to a type of spiritual initiation. It seems that life, as I had known it before, had ended, and yet a new life was beginning. It was a humbling experience. Never in my life had I been completely emptied, obliterated, and broken apart.

I surrendered everything I knew to that point. I was living out of a bag in my parent's home at that time. I slowly began to put my life back together. This time with ME being the one who decides what happens from here on out--no more giving my power away, no more putting others before me, no more living a life that was not my sovereign choice to live. I was being liberated, spiritually.

My journey of awakening has been riddled with challenges; however, you can't keep the light out for long. The power of the heart is more potent than any of the forces of this planet that wish to dominate and control us. Those forces that tried to destroy me just gave me the fuel I needed to strengthen my heart, transmute the pain, and purge all that was not in alignment with my soul's truth. The heart's inner knowing cannot be extinguished.

Truth, love, beauty, and freedom are the tenants of the heart. The heart is a force that cannot be contained and cannot be owned. Somehow flowers find a way to bloom through the asphalt, the lotus grows in the mud, and trees often grow through concrete.

I am a child of the divine, a Starseed, and as Starseed's, we know there is always a way.

Starseed Sayings:

"I suspect that we are all recipient of cosmic love notes, messages, omens, voices, cries, revelations, and appeals are homogenized into each day's events. If only we knew how to listen, to read the signs."

— **Sam Keen**

ABOUT THE AUTHOR

Michelle Kearney Lopez

Michelle is a Reiki Master Teacher, crystal healing practitioner, intuitive astrologer, oracle card reader, and holistic health advisor who emphasizes Ayurveda. Michelle teaches Reiki and crystal healing classes in her local area. Michelle is also an elementary school teacher with 23 years of teaching experience and a certified Yoga Alliance RYT200 Yoga Instructor. She is devoted to helping young children develop social-emotional skills to handle life's challenges through yoga and mindfulness in the classroom. She created a program in social-emotional learning and yoga for the classroom teacher, called The Heart-Centered Classroom. She plans to bring wellness to schools by sharing this foundation for wellness with other educators.

As an advocate for children's wellness, Michelle hopes that children will learn to embrace their own unique and natural expression. As our world shifts and changes, Michelle believes so does the way we guide our children into the future. By giving children the tools, they need to manage and regulate their own emotional climate, we are giving them skills they can utilize into their adult years. Collectively, we can help this next generation of new souls come into their own authenticity. They are the children of a New Earth, and they are unlike any we have seen so far. She believes this next wave of souls is going to need this extra emotional support so they can help create the New Earth that we are currently creating.

Michelle has currently authored a manuscript of a children's book called Animal Magic. She intends this book to be a foundational program in yoga and social-emotional learning where children can draw upon lessons from the natural world to help them integrate universal human values like compassion, courage, self-love, self-care, healthy boundaries, kindness, and resilience. Michelle has been a guest speaker at the Herbivore Festival in Yucaipa, and guest a yoga instructor at the Big Bear Yoga Festival.

When she is not teaching or doing healing work, she is mom to two growing teenagers, loves to hike and explore nature, paints mandalas, collects and digs for crystals, writes, and teaches children's yoga after school in her local community.

Michelle's intention for writing her story in Awakening

Starseeds is to help others with their own process of awakening. She hopes that someone will find their own experience mirrored in her story and will find some peace and healing from it. She also understands the ancestral healing of the voice can be experienced when we share our stories. Her belief is when we heal ourselves, we heal our past and future generations. Additionally, she understands the collective power of Starseeds coming together to share these stories. Michelle believes when we share these stories, it is entered into the Earth Akashic Record and will contribute to the liberation and healing of our planet.

For private healing sessions and classes, you can reach Michelle at sacredearth111@gmail.com,
michellelightbearer@gmail.com
Facebook-@sacredearth111
Instagram @sacredearth111
For mindfulness classes and children's yoga classes she can be reached at:
Facebook: @theheartcenteredclassroom,
theheartcenteredclassroom@gmail.com,
theheartcenteredclassroom.com,
Facebook: @heartcenteredyogaforkids

∾

Starseed Sayings:

"It takes great courage to see the world in all its tainted glory, and still to love it."
— **Oscar Wilde**

9

MY JOURNEY WITHIN

By RAZIEL FUENTEBELLA ARCEGA

During the financial crash of 2008 came the darkest hour of my life. What seemed like a perfect family with my "knight" turned into a nightmare.

My husband declared that he needed to find himself and figure things out on his own. He wanted to leave me, and he did. I was devastated. I felt abandoned with my two children, who needed continuous medical attention. I found myself left hanging on a thin vine with all my might having to figure out everything for myself.

With emotional shock and trauma, financial despair, confusion, and disbelief that this was happening to me, my heart broke into a thousand pieces.

What have I done? I was a full-time mom having to care for two children who have health issues. My first son, Nikolaus, had an autoimmune condition. He had a bad case of allergies/skin condition that resulted after his 3rd month of vaccination that ended up in UCLA for a six months study, doing white blood transfusions. It took two years of my life, observing my son's condition without much sleep.

On the other hand, my daughter Zarina had suffered from seizures and was diagnosed within the autism spectrum. Her speech wasn't developing until she got help from Special Ed speech classes. Obviously, I had to devote full-time care for my children's well-being at home, with a high risk of protecting their health issues while developing a mompreneur business to make ends meet.

Abandoned, I felt all alone. Time stood still. I did not know what to do after giving all my love and dedication to this relationship. I felt betrayed. Day and night, I walked around the house like a zombie. Rage, anger, and tears were pouring out of my being day and night. Helpless, I screamed, but no one heard me but my own ears. I was lost in a deep hole of darkness that felt as if I am being eaten away. I withered away, and people started to notice.

Despite having to fall into this deep dark hole, I knew I had to get back up to muster my strength and fortitude - face myself, my fears and provide care for my children. I recognized I needed much help too. It was the beginning of my healing journey. I wanted to find my spirit back and find a purpose.

I grew up as a Filipino Catholic. One day, a friend invited me a few times to a Christian discipleship program with a purpose to assist me in what my heart needed the most, fill in the void inside of me, to find God. And even after this program, the hunger for learning grew even more potent inside of me. On my own, I searched further. I kept seeing synchronized numbers, hearing divine messages, and felt an inclination to listen to my higher self, and I started to dig more.

In the meantime, I slowly but surely stepped into

building my business while balancing my home and work life. I asked God to send me clients to support me if he wanted me to keep going in this new direction of building my new life back.

I volunteered in the community, and it became a part of my therapy to give back. At the same time, I saw this opportunity to create my business network, which grew my customer base. When Mike and I met at a networking event, it later led me to meet Radhaa Nilia.

There was something special about Radhaa and her healing practice. I learned about Mike's story and had seen the results he had from his healings with her. I decided to go for a consultation with Radhaa. Her response, I needed a more in-depth type of healing, so she sent me to her mom, Maya The Shaman, for a "Lemurian Code Healing" session.

This was all fresh territory to me, and from where I came from, a traditional Catholic home, this is forbidden territory, like eating an apple from a forbidden tree. But at this time, I needed something profound, hands-on guide to getting me out of this rut. I was at my lowest, sad, lonely, depressed, doubtful, fearful condition, and I knew that if this works for me, I had a chance to make a quantum shift in my life, make things better.

I took my chance and courageously stepped into this unknown realm. I was ready for something different, something new, a journey of self-discovery. It's my way to enter this new frontier.

I met Maya The Shaman at their cozy healing house at Hollywood Hills. She scanned my body. Then she had told me to tell her my story and what brought me to her. I finally had someone to unload my substantial feelings. She listened with compassion. Then she had me lie down on her massage table without touching my body. She told me it's all energetic. I did what I was told. On the table, it was much more than what I had expected because the healing sent energy waves throughout my entire body. My body shook uncontrollably for quite some time. Then a split reality took place, I saw myself lying on the massage table looking down at me, and the swirling dark grey energy was leaving my body, moving out towards the nearby window, left into the ethers. I felt I was in a different dimension. She told me I just released seven generations' worth of bad karma and energies. I felt better after the session, smiling and glowing as the heavyweight lifted off me. I thanked Maya.

I continued to get sessions and worked closely with Maya for half a dozen years, bringing up many other new blockages or issues whenever they come up. She handled layers of blockages from past lives, business, entities, fears, doubts, and spirituality. I trusted the comfort zone we were in together.

I cannot forget my 10th session with Maya. It was October 6, 2013, a moment so deep and profound. To this moment in time, it brought tears and joy to my heart. It was my spiritual awakening.

I was very emotional that day. We did the usual protocol. But this time, it was over the phone. She started to say something I could not hear, nor understand, so I just relaxed. I let her do her work on me. I was almost falling into an altered state of consciousness when a vision came.

I was aware of my body, and as soon as the healing started, I saw a river flowing next to me. This river was very different and so beautiful. It continuously flowed with gold. Gold materials were everywhere, and it was endless. I started to pick up a bucketful of this gold, buckets after buckets. My daughter came first to help, then my son. My gaze went around the left side, where the stream was flowing into this bottomless pit of unlimited abundance. This place looked like paradise. It was Lemuria.

Then I slowly saw myself being lifted from the earth, viewing the aerial space insight. As I was being carried up from the ground, I can see it from a distance, slowly disappearing into the black space of the universe. I started to sob then cried because I felt a "Great" presence of *love* was beside me. I felt the fullest and purest *love* I had never felt before, and I said, "I know you love me, and I feel the fullness of your *love*, thank you!" I felt complete.

I stayed there in the presence of this "Grand Being." I thought I would drop back to earth; instead, I went the opposite direction. I started to see the galaxy, the stars, the formation of the universe's eye and saw the magnificence of it all. I stayed there staring back at its majesty, cosmic grandeur, feeling the pureness of love, the divine essence, the beginning of it all.

Suddenly, I heard the Creator say, "this is all for you." referring to the universe. "This is all yours (as in for everyone)." I cried from the very core of my heart. It was such a deep overwhelming feeling of love and gratitude.

As I was talking to God, I said, "I can't believe everything in the universe you created was accessible for me, all this beauty and grandeur, this feeling of serenity, peace, and pure love."

If this is Utopia, it was the ultimate place to be, with no worries nor concern, in perfect presence. I wanted to stay here. I was reflective and told Maya about my experience. The small part of me felt I exited out of my body. I was my true self, my spiritual self, no boundaries, in pure essence. Nobody, no arms, a cosmic being in a state of consciousness.

In the back of my mind, wow! How vast this universe is

compared to how tiny we are on this planet earth and how much more we can explore out there.

That was a remarkable and refreshing trip. Yet, to describe the feeling is difficult for me to express. I felt putting it in words will diminish its essence. But honestly, what a spiritual experience that was!

There is so much more that I had to explore, and with these fantastic cosmic experiences, each day is like unfolding and discovering this "divine" frontier, remembering who I truly am and how great *love* is.

I am humbled, grateful, and thankful!

Namaste.

ABOUT THE AUTHOR

Raziel F. Arcega

Raziel F. Arcega is a mompreneur, community leader, health, and wellness advocate. She is a certified minority woman small business owner with a professional background in advertising and promotions. Owner of LNR Promotions, her marketing and promotion company. She provides clients with high-quality service and products. Clients satisfaction is her priority. Raziel's motto: "Love, Nurture and Respect" ourselves, serve our community and our environment where we live in.

As a dynamic event organizer, she collaborates with various government agencies, Fortune 100, Fortune 500, non-profits, chambers of commerce, and other business associations. She aligns with non-conservative programs and sustainable related businesses such as health, wellness, fitness, and natural products.

For clean and sustainable business, Raziel is a professional coach and consultant in marketing-promotional strategies for alternative products and companies. Since 2008, Raziel is Involved in promoting natural health and wellness industry. An advocate in connecting and working with alternative healers, both Eastern and Western practitioners. She assists her clients' businesses grow. It is her heart's desire to create a healthy world for healthy and better living, a holistic lifestyle in mind, body, and spirit.

She has been a member, officer, board member, and ambassador for the Filipino Chamber of Commerce of Orange County since 2002. She created various business workshops and trade events with the Asian Business Association of Orange County, Orange County President's Council, NAAAP-OC, and other multi-ethnic community organizations in Orange County, Los Angeles, and Inland Empire. She's one of the co-founders, past president, and executive director of the Asian Business Association Inland Empire, creating a coalition among multi-ethnic leadership in the Inland Empire to grow and embrace a more united and robust networking environment for everyone in the business community to prosper.

She immigrated to New York from the Philippines in 1985 and received her Bachelor of Science Degree in Computer Science in 1990 with a master's in business administration Degree in 1993 from St. John's University, Jamaica, New York. Former President of the Filipino Society at St. John's. She co-founded the United Filipino Youth Council together with other student leaders from various schools in the New York/New Jersey/Connecticut area and a founding member of FIND, Filipino Collegiate Networking Dialogue, an East Coast coalition of student leaders. It expanded in several other states for the past 20+ years.

She moved to California in 1998, married Lyndon Arcega in 1999. Previous work includes Marketing Assistant at Citibank, Financial Analyst at Cornell University, Executive Marketing Assistant to the Senior Vice President at Time Warner/Warner Publishing, Inc. and Help Desk Marketing Analyst at BP/ARCO. Forced to stay home with their first son, owned LNR Enterprises in 2002, and branched off to LNR Promotions in 2005 with a growing customer base.

Raziel is a deeply passionate community leader, tree-hugger, "mompreneur" of two amazing children: Nikolaus (18 years) and Zarina (14 years).

links :-)
instagram.com/razielarcega
facebook.com/razielarcega
twitter.com/razielarcega
email: lnrpromotions@gmail.com

❦

"We began as wanderers, and we are wanderers still. We have lingered long enough on the shores of the cosmic ocean. We are ready at last to set sail for the stars."
— **Carl Sargan**

10

DISCOVERING THE DIVINE PLAN

By ROBERT RUBIN

I have always wondered if my life was meant for something greater. The Idea that I had a deeper purpose in this world has always been something I questioned within myself. Do I have a more vital role to play than just living day by day doing a 9 to 5 job to survive? My answer was always "yes," and if you answered the same, then you are not alone.

Since more than ever before in history, this phenomenon is happening more frequently every day -- ordinary people are beginning to realize that there are parts of their mind, body, and soul that go beyond the five senses. They are ready to make an even more significant impact and purpose in this world. Something more existed, something deeper and more fulfilling yet integral to one's existence. It is the part that does not bend to logic, reason, and even social conformity. It is more durable than any culture than any rule or any scientific fact. I call it "The Intuitive Within," and here I will share my story of how I discovered my own intuitive inside of me.

I recall the first time in my life when I was 18 years old, and I was at a crossroads between one of two paths. On one end was a life of security, as most people would call it, a stable job, working in my home country, earning a decent living. It's what most people said would be the best option. Since it offered what others would call a stable life, the other option existed within me since I was a boy. That option was to immerse me in the practice and lifestyle of the intuitive and the esoteric. In the early part of 1998, my choice was a scary and uncharted one. At the tender age of eighteen, I was given an opportunity. Choose "The Path" or stay in comfort.

I knew then what I know now. I could never give up who I was and my passion for bringing empowerment and clarity to others through the various gifts of the intuitive. Consequently, I chose "the path." Not knowing where it would lead me and how wild of a ride it would be. That was the moment! My "forging" from the universe began. Since it's only through fire that iron is sharpened, this would be my trial by fire.

From the intoxicating energies of my hometown of San Francisco, where all forms of lifestyle are accepted and celebrated, I was instantly sent to its literal polar opposite. A place I would call a natural wilderness still controlled by the conformity of dogma and religion with little options for me to grow. This place was in the Philippines. It was here that for ten years, I was asked time and time again by the universe. "Do you want this? Do you want the life that you committed to? Do you wish to continue?" Even with all the heartaches of losing loved ones, feeling alone and isolated, I continued to say yes.

Because who would I be if I were not me? From the beginning, I was ridiculed.

Most people would label me as "that weirdo guy" and would mock me. When I would tell the locals of my passion and dreams of building a thriving intuitive society built on acceptance and respect, most would laugh at me, saying it was impossible. I was often told I was out of my mind. There were times I thought that they were right. But I was choosing something beyond just me. I was accepting my Intuitive Truth. Despite all the trials that were sent my way to domesticate me and put me back to sleep, I chose to endure. I claimed my truth, and I said, *"I will live by it! Or, if need be, I will die by it! However, I will never give it up!"*

I continued my advocacy to help reach others like me with similar intuitive inclinations around the country through writing and correspondences. Through these efforts, Mysterium Philippines was created.

The more I endured, the more I realized that there were others like me, but many were in hiding as we were in a predominantly Catholic nation. Latent psychics, healers, empaths, witches, shamans alike were there, but all were keeping themselves hidden due to the fear of being ostracized.

After discovering this, I again committed to the path and to find the people who were like me. Those who felt alone, who needed to feel safe, and needed to find a place where they could belong. I would do this not only for myself but for every other person with spiritual gifts and abilities who felt alone in this country. I would commit to helping them find a permanent, loving, and supportive home.

"Something must have heard me or saw that I was ready because, by the end of 2007, my spiritual exile has ended. Without any planning and the resources to do so, I was sent to Metro Manila. It was then that I realized that the ten years in the province were meant to be a trial by fire. It would either make me quit or pressure cook me and condense my desire to build a thriving esoteric community in the Philippines into an unbreakable one. Now my intuitive within was completely unleashed."

Since that day, I have dedicated my life to reaching out to all forms of inherent potential around the country. Through the responsible uses of intuitive tools like the Tarot and a genuine desire to help my fellow brothers and sisters, I said in the words of Gandhi that I would 'be the change' in this world.

I was amazed to see so many people around the country who had potential. However, amongst the sheep lay many wolves who wished to take advantage of all this.

It was here that I discovered that the sacred masculine, the warrior, the soldier, the captain, would be the energy that I would need.

I would need to set an example of how practice should be and demonstrate that example in my everyday life. From an industry wrought with charlatanism and con artistry, I would choose to be one of the few who would never take advantage of the goodwill of any client, student, or client who would come my way. If I were not adding to their lives, I was not doing my job, and I would continuously say to myself.

As of this writing, I have discovered that my intuition within is what makes my life meaningful. It took a man with nothing to live for and gave him the things he always wanted. By following my intuitive truth, I was given a beautiful family when I previously had none. I was given a beautiful vocation of helping others grow in their inherent potential rather than working just a 9 to 5 job that I hated. It brought meaningful relationships into my life and has helped me whether some of the most challenging storms that life had to offer. It was all because I was committed to my intuitive truth.

I chose to articulate my experiences in my 2nd book, *The Intuitive Within* since I knew if others discovered this truth as I did, they would be of higher service to the world.

I have discovered that the intuitive truth of oneself is not polarized between light and dark in my journey. I understand that the existence of the light worker and the dark worker is necessary. The universe requires us as spiritual beings to embrace both sides.

I have seen some of the most sanctimonious light workers fall into sin, and I've seen some of the darkest souls do some of the most heroic and selfless things imaginable. It was here that I realized that only through accepting and incorporating both sides of the force that we complete ourselves as spiritual beings.

When I finally learned this, I realized the world needed to be consciously aware of the existence of duality, which makes us humans. It was here that I learned that we are beings of dual potentials, but naturally, we can gravitate towards either polarity or the other.

It has been part of my joy to help others celebrate the beauty of their intuitive selves. Be it light, dark, masculine, or feminine. Living in truth and a genuine fashion will only help awaken more the people around us than ever before.

Since then, Mysterium Philippines has become a home for people from all walks of life. Mysterium is living proof in the Philippines that one can live their intuitive truth and prosper. Respectively, we send out the call to people from all walks of life to come to join us in the knowledge that you have a home in Mysterium.

Starseed Sayings:

"Somewhere, something incredible is waiting to be known."
— **Carl Sagan**

ABOUT THE AUTHOR

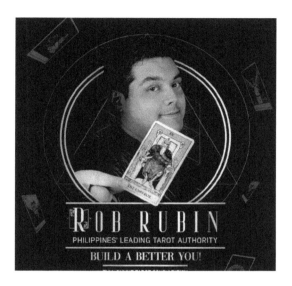

Robert Rubin

Robert Rubin is the founder of Mysterium Philippines Incorporated, the leading Intuitive Training Institution and Service provider in the Philippines. He has been hailed as the leading Tarot Authority in the Philippines with over 23 years of Practice and study. He has helped rebrand and professionalize the Practice of Tarot throughout the country through his game-changing Introduction to the Tarot program.

Rob is the author of, Defensive Occultism: A Handbook

of Supernatural Self Defense and The Intuitive Within. He has utilized his knowledge of the Practice and development of intuition to bring a greater awareness of the human potential and bring a better quality of living to those who join the Mysterium family. As an advocate of the responsible Practice of Spiritual arts, Robert has been featured across the Philippines and Internationally as one of the leading intuitive mentors and coaches from Metro Manila. Due to his advocacy, he has been featured in media outlets across the country and the History Channel itself during 2018's HistoryCon at the World Trade Center Manila.

As a professional tarot teacher and consultant at the Mysterium Philippines learning Centre, he has helped grow the Mysterium community to become the largest professional tarot organization in the country. He has personally instructed dozens of classes in the fields of Intuitive development and the Tarot since 2006 while dedicating the remainder of his focus as a professional Tarot consultant for over 20 years now.

He is happily married to his wife Sarah, the resident Reiki Master of Mysterium Philippines, and has two beautiful children Jacob and Nicole.

You may learn more about him at:
www.RobRubinReadings.com
www.IntuitiveWithin.com
www.facebook.com/RobRubinReadings
www.Instagram.com/RobRubinReadings

～

11

STARSEED MOM ON A MISSION

By CRISTAL ORTIZ

"Cristal, have a damn seat and listen because I've been trying to tell you for quite some time now that you must awaken."

It started as a typical day. I went to the gym with a friend, stopping to eat on my way to visit my sister. I became nauseated, pulling into her driveway. Exiting my car, I started vomiting on her front lawn. She took me inside to the sofa before making my way to the bathroom to vomit again. I had just been saying how good I'd felt lately, so I could not understand where or how I became sick? The vomiting continued for about an hour on and off, complete with visual distortions moving, spiraling as if I was drunk. Laying on the ground slowed the spinning; moments later, I left my body and saw myself lying on the bathroom floor from above while fully aware. I could see myself lying on the floor and stared at myself as I was breathing slowly on the floor.

My sister came into the bathroom to check on me and asked me if I was ok? I tried to respond, but no words would come out. I nodded when she asked if I wanted to go to the hospital. The Paramedics arrived. I was still mute and experiencing body paralysis, much like sleep paralysis. It was scary, but I remained calm, focusing on my breathing and watching the medics do their job. They asked me questions and tried to help me sit up. I could not answer or hold myself up. I just melted off the chair. Tears of frustration on my face. I was unable to communicate outside of sighs, nods, and head shakes. A pen wouldn't even stay in my hand to write. I remained in this paralytic state for hours.

My bloodwork came back normal. I was scheduled for a CAT scan, and while waiting in the hallway on my hospital bed, something inside told me to try to move my toes, and they moved! After feeling trapped in my own body, I could finally wiggle my fingers too. After a few minutes, I was able to get myself to sit up and even made it to the bathroom alone. My voice returned also. Before the CAT scan, which came out normal, while paralyzed, the doctor had asked my sister and mother if I was under a lot of stress lately, to which I nodded, and they agreed - yes, for years, since the day he left me.

I was seven months pregnant with our second child that night when my husband walked out on me. Zero remorse crushed me as he justified his actions by reminding me there were plenty of single mothers out there. We had our differences, sure, every couple does, but I never expected him to leave me alone to care for our two young children, one not even born.

I'd had hints at times, something urging me to wake up, not to take him back, but I had ignored my intuition for the sake of the family. I could not ignore it any longer. Everything was tumbling and crumbling down on me, much like the tower card in the tarot. My spirit refused to be ignored any longer. I would be forced to face every fear and dark part of my mind. I struggled with the last two months of pregnancy, working, keeping up with bills. I felt so alone. My mother made nasty comments about how stupid I was for having another baby with him. I started to loathe the impending birth because although the pregnancy was hard, I knew caring for a toddler *and* a newborn would be even harder.

My daughter was born on March 7, 2015, via c-section. Gratefully my cousin Bianca came to be with me in the operating room and offered me the unconditional love and support I was getting nowhere else. However, I was still trying to cope with the loss of my relationship with their father. I questioned how he could be so present for our first baby and yet not for the second? I experienced feelings of abandonment and unworthiness. All the why's and what if's as endless thoughts kept replaying in my head. Not only was I healing physically from the c-section, caring for a new baby and toddler alone, paying bills, and working with no maternity leave, but I felt no emotional support from my mother, who was emotionally cold and cruel.

Postpartum depression consumed me, complete with visions of self-harm, not of doing it, but of the aftermath. Never in my life had I experienced such frightening thoughts. Every time I got a little sleep, I would see myself from an astral plane - with an empty bottle of my prescribed Percocet's. I would be unresponsive as my children were alone and in distress, with nobody else there to care for them. The visions made me fear sleep. Only the love I have for my girls kept me from being consumed by the darkness. I admit I found it hard to connect with my new baby. It wasn't that instant love at first sight like with my first daughter. I was on autopilot after giving birth, and our bonding was delayed. I had to grow to love her. Although I never had thoughts of harming her, it was hard to love her at first when I felt no love from anyone or for myself. How much I hated their father. I felt consumed with unforgivable feelings for his choice. His selfishness felt it robbed me of the motherly ability to bond with my new baby. I felt injustice for my child and resentment toward him, and my heart grew so much darkness. Emotionally, I hit rock bottom.

A few months later, I filed for divorce and enrolled in a Paralegal program. I did whatever I could to remain "busy" and mask the pain. I knew I wasn't allowing myself to heal by doing these things. I thought I had everything under control. My divorce proceeded in my favor until the night before the final hearing. My car broke down. I missed my court date, and the judge reversed everything to favor their father. My children were taken away from me and sent to live with him. They were given to the very person who had walked out on them.

The darkness and anger I already harbored multiplied tenfold. Since he walked out, the dark nights of the soul deepened and became darker after my children were taken away. I had zero desire to do anything other than work to make money for an attorney so I could fight for my children.

Around two months later, a stillness came over me and, with it, an attempt to rationalize with myself about the situation. I allowed the dark feelings in and recognized them individually to allow healing as I became aware of how toxic my inner realm had become. I slowly started to think positively about the situation. My children living with their father for six months allowed me time and space to finally face all that I was suppressing inside. I saw how strong I had been for them, always able to care for them despite my inner turmoil. My ex's time with the children offered him a chance to see what being a single parent with two kids was like and allowed the baby to bond with her dad.

As mothers, we tend to put our very own healing and feelings to the side to care for our children, even when we need healing ourselves, but my alone time granted me much-needed healing space. It allowed me to learn to forgive him. I came to realize that if I did not forgive him, then the universe would not let me have my children back. It was the most humbling and painful thing I've ever accomplished in my life. Thinking back in the emergency room, after my CAT scan results, I was told I had a severe anxiety attack, which can mimic many other health conditions. I believed the diagnosis at the time. But looking back, I know it was not an anxiety attack at all! My soul had had enough and was forcing me to listen, to forgive everything and everyone. To let go and trust. To give me everything I need so I may thrive, to seek a new path.

By April 2017, our custody agreement had become 50/50, and I was so thrilled to have my babies back! We developed a better co-parenting relationship and began to make the best of it. A new life was unveiling itself for me. I became a vegan, started meditating, consulted my crystals, practiced patience, used amazon plant medicines, and much more.

Most importantly, I have become a better mother to my daughters. I am teaching them things I was never taught, especially self-love and establishing a connection with the earth and moon. I am on a journey of self-healing that will bleed out into my daughters and heal all of us and generations after. It is the most sacred work I feel a mother can do for herself and her children.

I have still got a long way to go. However, I am ever so grateful to the divine for sending me lessons of the darkness, for there cannot be a day without a night.

ABOUT THE AUTHOR

Cristal Ortiz

My name is Cristal Ortiz, living in Florida, and I am so happy to be a part of this book. It is quite flattering and an honor to have my story be heard. Out of the thousands of people that Radhaa has on her Instagram page she connected with me. I am just a mom, why me? Then I thought, Moms are completely underrated, we have the most essential job of humanity. Sometimes, our most significant contribution to the universe may not be something that we do, but someone we raise.

I have two daughters, a dog, two cats and a small business owner of my own cleaning service, with one of my sisters. However, my TRUE passion is helping others, and I am an affiliate for a company that sells mucoid plaque cleanses, phase Body Cleanse. I am not a paid employee, again this is just a passion of mine. I help to motivate, coach, as well as lead by example for others to cleanse their bodies of disease and lead healthier vegan lifestyles.

I enjoy reading, yoga, meditation, weightlifting, spending time with my children, grounding with the earth, and many other things that make my inner being joyful.

————————

I can be found on Instagram and FB promoting this cleanse. Instagram @cristal_aa. Please feel free to reach out for cleansing or transitional tips to becoming vegan, I love to help.

～

12

AWAKENING TO LIFE'S PURPOSE

By KARUNA CHINCHKHEDE

"We Come Here with Mission. We Come Here with Purpose."

My life path was set when I completed my Quantum Healing Hypnosis certification. Though I received guidance from my guides, I did not imagine changing my life forever.

The first practice session was on my husband, which made me question my choice of learning a hypnosis-based healing modality.

The second session was with a client with path-breaking results. Dolores Cannon used the term *"volunteer"* in her book *"Three Waves of Volunteers and The New Earth."* My client had asked questions about her being a volunteer on Earth. Her higher self (HS) answered *'Yes,'* confirming that she is a volunteer and then added, *"So are you."* Are you referring to me? *"In this particular lifetime, I volunteered to help the Earth ascend to a higher dimension and help humanity make a similar move towards their own ascension."*

After that session, that day, I drove back home in a state of pure joy. I knew that this was my path, and this was my purpose. I was given a picture in my meditation about my role wherein I was standing holding a lamp on my head, and people were rushing somewhere. It was explained that they were rushing to the new Earth, and I was showing them the way.

"What is my life purpose?" – a question asked by everyone coming to me for their session. As humans living in 3rd density, we want to know our calling in life and plan the next step to move forward. Knowing what answer lies in the future helps our 3D journey. So, during our session, I ask my client's higher self to show a picture of how their future looks like so that they can look forward to it.

A client's higher self explains how knowing the life purpose makes the client consciously feel, *"She feels now she has a purpose. She felt before her life was boring, with no purpose. Now she has a lot to do."*

It was so true for me. As the path started unfolding for me, I truly began to live my life. For the very first time, I was able to tell what my passion was. I did not know that before. Like my clients, I go into hypnosis myself. Like them, I do not have an awareness of what is going on in my physical surroundings. I know now that it is that powerful to do my mission work.

The biggest draw for Quantum Healing (QH) session is to receive guidance from our own higher self. In QH sessions, we directly access the inner wisdom called higher consciousness, higher self, our connection to divine source creator. A person's infinite wisdom gets a voice and directly talks with my client's conscious self. I find it very empowering to see that my clients hear their own knowledge residing within them. As more of us awaken to our true selves, the QH session is a great way to initiate our inner journeys and begin self-discovery.

Let me give you examples of several clients who tapped into their higher selves and its outcome.

Most of the clients I have found in my sessions are Lightworkers, Healers, and Conduits of Energy, and that is their life's purpose. In a brief period of 3 years of my journey as a QH practitioner, I came across many evolved souls in physical bodies, living an ordinary 3D life and yet doing great healing work for the planet and the whole of humanity.

They are the champions of light. Some are awake already. While others are coming out from their amnesia, trying to find answers, their divine self continues to wake them up to their ultimate purpose on Earth. Their divine self also guides them towards other practitioners and me to get their life mission going.

In QH sessions, client's physical bodies are prepared to connect with their higher self. Physical activities like yoga, being in nature, breathwork, meditation, and the right diet advise the body to take on its purpose. The emotional, mental bodies are prepared by releasing fears, pains, doubts, negative emotions, etc. The healing work continues even after the session.

One time, a powerful message from a client's higher self came through, saying, *"She has to heal the planet."*

"She has the energy in her hands, and she has the energy in her soul. She is the divine energy, and we want her to heal this planet. She was sent here to fight, to control this planet so that the demons will not be here. There are too many negative forces on this planet. There are so many working against what we as spiritual beings want to do on this planet. Mother Earth, the beautiful Gaia, needs all the help she can get."

I listened as her higher self continued to say, *"She is to

pull out the map or get a globe, and she is to place her hands in certain regions and send the energy of love. She is to release the entities that are walking on this planet. It is time to release these entities, and it is time for her to take her place as a healer of this planet because that is why she is here. She is here to heal this planet, to raise the energy levels of those are on this planet by using the maps."

Her higher self goes on, *"Because even though humans do not feel the energy grids on this planet, they are here. We can manipulate it and control it because dark forces control it because no one is working the energy fields, no one is working the energy grid. She is one of the millions that have that capability. Her job is to clear the energy fields on this planet."*

I listen as her higher self continues, *"She is then contacting those other beings that are on this planet that have this purpose. They will all work in connection with each other, and they will heal the mother earth. They will heal beautiful Gaia. That is why she is here. That is her mission, and that is her purpose. She must release the souls that are trapped on this planet. Because they are affecting the energy grids around this planet."*

Her higher self gives the action plan on how the planet can be healed. *"Take the globe, put your hands on the globes, envision in your mind's eye the energy grids on the planet, and send energy through your hands as energy healers. Many people should be doing this. You (referring to me) can also do it."* Her higher self commands, *"Start healing certain areas on the maps, like feuding countries, the places with famines, countries under war or war-like situation. That is how Gaia can be healed."*

During another session with my client, the next one I discovered has to do with what I call "Transmuters of Darkness."

Some wonder why they attract darkness. Humans experience it in their everyday lives in the form of alcohol, substance abuse, working at places like casinos. They are divinely placed at such sites to bring light to darkness and its inhabitants. They wonder why some unknown people pour their hearts out to them because they have an ability, an intense light that can transmute this darkness.

A client's life purpose conversation with her higher self goes like this: *"She will be brought to people who are carrying darkness so that the darkness can be exposed in her presence as she carries the light within. She is not to judge this. She just needs to allow for others to be uplifted by her energetic presence, which causes the truth to automatically come out of everyone around her. Eventually, events will happen that will bring out these shadows, and she must only allow the process to happen. She should stand there and say nothing; just allow the light codes to infuse it to others. It will help other persons in their time of silence and in their dreams to fully integrate the light codes and erase the shadow so that it isn't transmitted into any other for the shadow seeks to expand itself. Still, it is darkness, and it cannot survive in the presence of light."*

Here is another encounter I had with a client. It is all about, "Just Be, as Healers."

Many have incarnated just to be. Others heal only by being present. Some don't even need to learn anything to help others. Some are advised to learn new methods. Some have chosen to work in the field of medicine etc., so that they can directly work with people who need this service. Each one is fully supported by their souls and their cosmic families at every step in their life purpose.

Her higher self started to speak, *"Her mission is to just be, and whatever she chooses is fine. It's her energy signature that comes through the things that she does."*

"Does she do anything for others?" I asked. Her higher self responded, *"She can do whatever she wants to do. It is all okay. There is nothing that she must do. Just be there, being wherever she is, she is contributing to the light grid. She is already doing what she needs to do. Everything else is just elective."*

Then there are other versions of one's purpose, *"Resting in Life."*

Not everyone here is on a big mission or to learn lessons. For some, this life is a relaxing time and to just have fun. To help others learn from their experiences. Some have taken up a job to guide their family and friends.

Another client's conversation with her higher self is, *"To have a good home with someone she loves, with a little business, with family and friends, kids and one or two dogs."*

I also noticed that when a client has many more lessons to still learn in their current life, their life purpose is not clear or not yet revealed. If the lessons are already learned from a specific situation, a particular relationship, but the soul is still hanging on to it, their higher self would quickly clear the connection. If the soul must do the work by themselves, the action plan is given. They must work on it until the next path is revealed to them.

ABOUT THE AUTHOR

Karuna Chinchkhede

Karuna Chinchkhede is a Quantum Healing Hypnosis Technique (QHHT) Level 2 practitioner. She is also trained in other hypnosis-based healing modalities like Introspective Hypnosis, Genesis Healing, and Beyond Quantum Healing (BQH), and Angelic Universal Regression Alchemy (AURA). She uses Quantum Healing Hypnosis as a tool to access higher consciousness for healing mind, body, and spirit. With her work, she is committed to helping others to find their own light, discover who they truly are, and set them on their path of empowerment and inner wisdom.

Contact Information:
www.karunachinchkhede.com
www.quantumhealers.com/karunachinchkhede
www.qhhtofficial.com/members/karuna-chinchkhede

13

REIGNITING MY GALACTIC SOUL

By ARRAMEIA AURAIRE ARAISS

Midst my contemplation about how many times I've been in the hospital this year, the doctor comes in to check my drip. With a serious tone, he says: "Given the results, I recommend you stay for 15 days (about 2 weeks). "Me: "What?!? No way!? I have a video shoot tomorrow!"

The doctor looks at me as if I'm mad. He repeats that I have a severe problem with my kidneys, and if I leave tomorrow, I am risking death. I am thinking yeah whatever, how many times they are going to tell me that as a safety warning and when is it actually severe?

"Could you give me some pills to take, so I can shoot the video and come back?" I ask casually. The doctor is all shocked and puzzled by my behavior. Let me sign a reverse, gives me pills, and get picked up to go home.

En route my "career - superstar brain" switches on. How the fuck am I gonna be on camera tomorrow when my face is all puffy? Calling my facialist. She recommends dipping my face in a bucket of ice with cucumbers. Ok, on it! Stopping to get ice. Tick. Stuff for hair, make up all organized. Tick. Last issue on my mind. Wait! How am I gonna do all the choreography when I can hardly walk?! Shit sticks!!

Also, what sucks is that I have this dick of a director doing this music video. He seemed like a nice guy at the start, then did not want my stylist on the shoot and other weirdness. I was puking midst dance rehearsals, and he did not even comment on it ... not one word!! Like, are you ok or something ...? Nope. Just said, "Back to position," I mean wtf?!!! This is the first time I'm not directing or co-directing my own video. We even have an extra production company involved, and I'm like... not fukkin used to this. Anyway, ...it is just one day of shooting and ...uhm many days of editing, grading, ...and THEN I'm done with it! :-)

I just got back to my warehouse (I live in a serene artistic community in London). My manager arrives to discuss tomorrow and asses my state. What if the doctor was right and I'm really going to die? I'm wondering. It is clear that I will not be able to dance. In an alternate reality, where I'm not a slave to my art, I could go back to the hospital and actually get better!? But we have already paid for it. We have actors, makeup, hair and fashion stylists, photographers, film crew, etc.

Here is a solution! An extra dancer will do it instead of me. I'm relieved yet annoyed. I worked on my dance piece for a month! My manager makes some calls. I go to sleep, hoping that I will wake up in some sort of a usable state. Energy drinks by my bed. Ice bucket ready to go. Alarm for 5am. Let us do this!

When I get to the shoot, the director is looking at me as if I'm some sort of a diva that is just making shit up about my health and creating drama. Seriously? If I am to be worrying about this dick, I'll not shoot it today, so fuck him.

Luckily, I have my lovely assistant here helping me to move around the set.

The first scene is being an empress, so at least I have a throne to sit on. On the side, royal refreshments: Nurofens and energy drinks.

I'm usually rather good on camera. This time, however, I can hardly open my eyes and wondering how the fuck am I gonna do this? I just rest on the throne until the red light goes on.

While I wait, it dawns on me! I can call on the galactic beings, that I reconnected with recently!?

A few weeks ago, I received some kind of DNA activation. Since then, I connected with my galactic family. One afternoon I spontaneously transported to some higher realm. I appeared amongst otherworldly crystalline light beings. Telepathically transmitted frequency and geometry codes were a means for communication. Strangely, the place felt more familiar to me than Earth. A world created out of high vibrational thoughts, love, purity, and breathtaking beauty. As I acknowledged my light body, knowledge started to pour forth. My galactic name was revealed. My original intention, why I came to Earth, was brought to my attention. Liberating and healing the human race was the core of my purpose. This powerful reminder got me questioning whether all the music stuff I do on Earth is actually as useful as I thought.

Didn't think about it since being back on Earth. Not only I'm always on shoots, gigs, or in the studio, but also my best friend and beloved grandma recently died. Lately, I don't seem to have time to process much of anything.

"Camera ready, take one!" shouts the director.

I'm calling on my galactic family to help me so I can gracefully convey this archetype. I let go and allow their energy to flow through me. It feels as if I'm just watching myself perform. I am gently uplifted, and it seems to be working. Dick of a director is super impressed, people on set are clapping, and I'm focused on getting a sip of energy drink before the next take. Filled with immense gratitude for my unseen helpers.

Afternoon. Just finished another look change. My vision is foggy. Locating the camera is tricky. It's very tragic this whole event. So terrible and ridiculous, that I find it funny. By now, I have had 5 Nurofens, 4 energy drinks, and my assistant is almost carrying me around. What I find fascinating about the entertainment industry is how cold everyone is. Too cool to be nice? Yeah, the star is half dead. Normals. Like some type of "all these stars are fucked up" mentality.

Last take, and I'm "going" home. I can't be bothered to take off any makeup or anything, so I just leave as I am. I want to be by myself. Had enough of people and pressure for the day.

I'm walking through my cold warehouse hallway, trying to find keys. Next thing I know, my friend is looking at me from the top. The vague notion that I'm lying on the floor slowly creeps into my exhausted brain.

My manager comes to pick me up. I'm swollen everywhere, my whole body hurts. He thinks I should fly to Prague, where I had my kidney operation. "What's gonna happen to the radio campaign when I'm not here?" I worry. Luckily, he's one of the people who are actually sane and cares about me. He says, "There is absolutely no point to radio campaigns now or in the future if you're dead. You need to get your health together first". I'm relieved and annoyed because I've worked so fukkin hard to get to where I am now. It took me so many years of nonstop work to have this level of the team. Things are finally starting to happen on a bigger scale. All of this momentum is now going to shit, cuz my body is not up for it. Argghh!!!

Prague. After the eternity of 10 days, I'm released from the hospital. Much fun for a workaholic.

Dying mode over. Still feeling pretty rough. Body aches weirdly. Range of motion for my neck is about 5mm each side. New kid on the block - killer migraine. Pills to take, many. Prescription reads 14 days of bed rest. Yeah right. I will be resting while editing the video with the dick of a director. (I should really forgive this guy by now).

My head hurts as if I'm repeatedly electrocuted. In this state, giving feedback on an edit is like painting blindfolded. We are already late on the agreed delivery date, and I'm really starting to hate my career.

Despite my ignorant arrogance, my body's determined to demonstrate it's need for rest. R.I.P.? My body's strike manifests as a "can't get up no more - I'm sick - kinda dying - vertigo -fog all the time" state.

Eventually, I surrender, and I just live in a bed. For days. Days and nights become one blur. Awake times weaved into dream states.

Only my heart's call cuts through the haze. A loud and clear call to a higher service and a deep yearning to let go of my career in entertainment. Irresistible pull to let the light being within me unleash. Inner knowing it's time to explore my Starseed origins and connect with my galactic family on Earth.

My head wants to continue building upon my recent success in the music industry. I've come so far already!

This head - heart split is causing me physical pain. Completely non-compatible paths. One is sharp left, another one sharp right. Nothing in between.

After those thoughts, I get into a state of complete blackout. What has been happening the last few days?! Have I been dead, alive, or somewhere else? No memory. No recollection of anything at all.

Right now, I'm sitting in a tearoom with my dear friend, who is a healer and a musician. Very advanced soul, boundlessly loving, joyful, and peaceful. He always knows what direction to send me to support my highest soul journey. Tonight's healing is focused on adjusting my blocked neck. Right away, I flow into a deep state of awareness. The world around me is slowly dissolving. Until all of a sudden, a flash of light enters.

A flash of light turns into continuous streams of light waterfalls pouring into my entire body with great force. All my cells are being filled up with intense highly charged potent light. My vibration keeps increasing. My body feels bigger yet weightless. As if a whole new light being had just entered my body. Midst the continuous influx of this new light, the former observer dissolves. I am now this light being. Pulsing and vibrating with pure light essence. Held by a commanding presence. Feels like coming home yet being on a foreign planet.

As Petr talks, it generates beautiful multi-colored sound waves with frequency codes. Energy fields of people and objects are overlapping, dimensions weaving into one another. Various hues of emotions, vibrations, and thought forms floating in space. Elements intertwining.

It's time to go. Walking in this new avatar feels a little strange. It is easier to make more extensive steps and amble. Earth's hologram is quite intricate yet still dense. It seems that a lot of various kinds of beings live here. An exciting place worth exploring.

We walk onto the main square and just stand there

watching the concert of energies. After seeing the prevalence of fear, guilt, shame, and other disruptive frequencies, the reason behind my appearance here is crystal clear. It is to be a pure vessel for source love and assist in liberating the human race. Mainly to help install and stabilize the 5D consciousness and build the high vibrational grids around the Earth. After that, more beings can move into the new vibrant, loving, joyful, and miraculous grid-hologram.

Petr nods with deep insight and understanding, I telepathically nod back pulsing with love and gratitude, we start walking towards new realities. The flowing lightness in this new avatar is enjoyable, and so is creating pretty holograms from thought-forms.

Shortly after this significant rebirth moment, I became a very joyful full-time healer, spiritual teacher, and started combing music with healing at sound events. I do this work to this day while integrating the "new being" that I am now, with my past.

Music video described at the beginning of this chapter YouTube: Veronika Vesper - Glory Box.

The rest of my even more fun and fascinating adventures after this rebirth moment can be found in my upcoming book, *"Mission Earth."*

Starseed Sayings:

"When we have completed all the journeys and adventures through our variety of lives, we are supposed to return to the Creator with our accumulation of knowledge. It is then absorbed. In this way we are considered cells in the body of God."

—**Dolores Cannon**

.

ABOUT THE AUTHOR

Arrameia Auraire Araiss

Arrameia Auraire Araiss is an awakened Starseed, spiritual teacher, energy healer, coach, author, vocalist, sound code creatress, and a performance artist on a mission to help Starseed's awaken their superpowers, higher consciousness, into bliss, so we can come together liberate the human race.

Successfully guiding ambitious Starseeds, leaders, and big-hearted entrepreneurs on their journey to awakening, via transformative coaching and intuitive energy healing. She helps clients to transition from unfulfilling life in the matrix to a blissful awakened life. She is also nurturing and certifying the next generation of healers as a teacher of the super powerful Theta Healing Technique®.

Arrameia is currently working on a memoir book called Mission Earth, which tells the story of her Starseed activation and transitioning from a career in the music industry (as singer-songwriter-performer under the name Veronika Vesper) as a full time "Starseed worker."

14

BE EMBODIED

By BYRON BRADLEY CARRIER

B arely beyond high school, I came face-to-face with death and birth, working for a funeral home that also ran the local ambulance. I dealt with old dead bodies, and on the ambulance, watched some die, saved a few from death, and helped deliver a slippery baby. At eighteen, I saw more raw death and life than most ever see.

Sparing you the rawness of embalming, I will share how the rude reality of bodies got me to wondering and admiring. The inside parts are really there, just like they say in the anatomy books, functioning correctly while we don't notice. It works all our lives on our behalf. The miracle of a baby coming out of a mother awed me. That it goes on to develop ability, language, song, psychology, and a life story enthuses me.

In college, subjects I had avoided, like chemistry, awakened an appreciation in me for organized, accumulated, ever refined scientific knowledge. Anatomy was the most interesting. We run our brains on top of an astonishing assemblage of intricate and elaborate interconnections, all enmeshed in an ecosystem of support. We are much more interdependent with bodily and worldly realities than we tend to appreciate and actualize. We are natural bodies of a limited duration living in an ecosystem responsive to how we treat it. We might better love and celebrate our bodies and our ecosystem than take them for granted or imagine we are apart from either.

It seems an insult to the Creator to ignore, deny, disparage, and waste our own bodily incarnation. Living well in our frame fully, happily, healthily, ethically, and gratefully seems a better use of our precious bodies than any asceticism or judgmental shame. We are our bodies, at least for now.

Funeral directing led me to seminary. Dealing with dead bodies and grieving families is only a part of the more holistic challenge and opportunity we have as humans. Ministry helps people live well while also trying to help society be healthy and fair. It deals with everything from pregnancy to death to beyond. The liberal ministry has a much broader concern than whether to merely believe in various scriptures, dogmas, and authorities. It affords and affirms our right to be smart, to be skeptical of fantastic wishful thinking, imposed as if God's truth.

Chief among these is the expectation that I, as a minister would confidently affirm other-worldly realities such as living on past death. It's what ministers are expected to do. Much of the world cling to this feeling or belief that we transcend to some other place, or into some new body. I know of no such situations or events. In all my embalming, I never saw the ghost of a soul. The body no longer seemed to be the persons, but if and where the person was – I don't know. Insisting they must be somewhere is like asking when we blow out a candle whether the flame still burns. It doesn't. It just is not. It was, and it isn't.

Similarly, I suspect when we die, we don't even know we're gone. There is no loss, for there is no one there to notice. The living knows loss; theirs is the grief. But the one who passed? Probably less aware of it all than when we utterly lose our self in a deep sleep. Eternal torment or reward? Endless incarnations until we get it right? Like Lucretius, I can't say those are true. I won't say it if I don't know it.

More critical than after-life or instead-of-life is this life we're given. Those who never appreciated or fulfilled being born want to pine for something better? A cosmic creation forms and supports them, yet they are not satisfied, praying to a Creator for "more" or "other"? Is this world a little testing ground, a stepping-stone, to a supposed other? When comes gratitude for what we're given, or responsibility, or celebration?

As eldest of five children, I had been raised Catholic but had left it at age 14. I went face-to-face with the friendlier priest to confess and stop my sin: to keep coming when I no longer believed in it. Circumcised and baptized as an infant, I learned the Catechism, taught not only the right answers but the right questions. Allegedly. Supposed truths taught by authorities based on traditions rooted in what someone said someone else said long ago didn't stir or convince me. I had my own questions and answers to explore and live up to. So, I left.

Later, after seminary, my disappointment with western religion's ignoring our bodily place in a worldly ecosystem was doubled in India. While *maya* can mean merely an *illusion* – mistaking a rope in the corner for a snake, the extreme version of *maya* – that we are *not* the body and the world *isn't* as real or meaningful as some supposed high state – seemed to me to *cause* and *allow* poverty and suffering. Whole communities live in diseased filth, yet it's rationalized as temporary karma. A temporary predicament, yes, but a deserved one? Merely an illusion? Suffering? So what?

It seems flippant to use the body to say we aren't the body. We hear the message via our bodies. It rides in our bodies. When we wake up from sleeping, we wake up in our bodies, not next to it, not in some other place. When someone dies, we no longer can hear their perspective, and someone must deal with the body.

So, when I, sickened, had the close darshan of Shri Rajneesh in Bombay in 1972, he all jeweled and adored, I wanted to punch him in the nose. He went on about how we are not our body, and about a mile from there, a thousand bodies lived in "houses" made of tin and cardboard, all sharing one water spicket and having no toilet. I did not dislike him, but I wanted to test his privileged, smug stance. "If the world is merely *maya*, and if we are not the body, would you mind if I punch you again?" I would ask.

(Of course, I did not. "May he be reborn into that nearby scrappy slum into a life of hunger, mud, and pain," I thought. Then I took it back. *Ahimsa* (non-injury) is for *all* beings, even him. And later, I came to admire his bold teachings.)

Going to India was one culture shock; returning to the U.S. was a worse one. It is one thing to see all the beggars, the rivers fermenting from all the feces floating in them, the flies, and vultures. It is another to see fat, frantic people suffering from the glut of frivolous consumerism, oblivious to the murderous war our military waged to protect us from falling dominos, utterly unaware or uncaring of what our sudden short-term civilization was doing to long-term Mother Earth.

How can we honor the Creator without loving Creation? What if we believed the creation myth on page one of the Bible, Genesis One? The one where the Creator not only generates an evolving, natural world, complete with plants, animals, and humans (males and females) in six stages but, importantly, also calls it "good" and advises us to "replenish" it? How good would we get, would Creation get, if we were to love and replenish what is originally and ultimately good? How healthy? How fulfilled? How good could we and it get?

Such gurus seemed as inadequate and misleading as some priests and popes had. When will our religions direct our care to our bodies, each other, and our ecosystem? These are our home and family. Aren't we in and of these – at least?

Our bodies and the world are made of elements formed in an earlier exploding star. The initial one had only the smallest components. When it went supernovae, it created all the larger molecules that make the earth and our bodies possible. Add in seemingly endless eons of effort and accomplishment via selection and evolution. We are built to accumulate success. Every organism was the reincarnation of earlier forms, only improved in some way. None of our forebearers failed at staying alive long enough to pass on their form. We are structured of success.

What we think of as human history is only the recent part of a much longer event. We might be, not at the end, but in the early eons of living on far, far longer.

But how? In love with life, or not?

We might be more, but we're our bodies at least, and that is a lot. We are each a unique incarnation of a good

Creation. We have interior bones, lungs, eyeballs, hands, hearts, and minds. We can live, love, wonder, and adventure. Our bodies and earth are home base for whatever else we might be. We live in social systems and an ecosystem that can be exhausted or exalted. I'm for our embodying our awakened star seed selves as ethically, beautifully, healthily, and successfully as we can while we can.

ABOUT THE AUTHOR

Byron Bradley Carrier

Byron Bradley Carrier was born in Pontiac, Michigan, on
Hiroshima Day. He was a licensed funeral director before

becoming a Unitarian Universalist minister, which he has practiced for 50 years. He provides commentary, ceremonies, and counseling, all available through his website. You can read more of his life and writings, contact him, or acquire his services at:

www.earthlyreligion.com

15

THE SACRED AKASHIC RECORDS

By TEZA ZIALCITA

I grew up in the beautiful and magical country of the Philippines staring at the stars nightly by the bay window, knowing that the stars are my home. I did not feel like I belonged here. I was always questioning human beings and why they are not sensitive and kind towards each other and living things.

At the age of two, I had a near-death experience in the hospital. I was diagnosed with Diphtheria. I saw my body and my Mama holding me, and there was an oxygen tent beside us. My two brothers were running in the hallway. This vision was surreal, and it created an imprint in my cellular memory. It was the beginning of my spiritual journey.

Growing up, I felt that I was connected to a higher force. My third eye was open.

I could see spirits when I was nine years old. My late grandmother and cousin appeared right before my eyes. I realized I had these spiritual gifts. I started prophesying, seeing the future of my family members. My mediumship was pronounced as I experienced a lot of visitations from the spirits. My huge family of 10 was fascinated by my unique gifts, and they were there to support me.

Yet, life has multiple ways for me to experience it. I've had a lot of dark nights of the souls. The most current one was in 2017 when I lost my 33-year old son Theo to suicide. It was traumatic, as we did not expect this to happen within our family. Theo was able to donate 4 of his organs to help save others' lives.

The other was having been a victim consciousness I experienced from the sexual abuse I suffered from my father and other men when I was young. I was married young, and I had four children. I found freedom from my abusive relationship at the age of 36 when I finally left my marriage.

As I continually searched for the meaning of my life, in 2008, I studied the Akashic Records. On the first day of learning the Akashic, I awoke from my sleep and felt hands scanning my body energetically. Then I heard a loud voice, "You are returning home." I was in shock when I woke up. I asked myself, is this a sign that I am going to die today? I did not know what home was, and now, I realize it was my soul. Returning home is where the Akashic Records are.

My soul's journey has been recorded in my book of life. It was the beginning of my ascension process.

I was on a massage table receiving a Reiki treatment while a surreal vision came. My guides were showing me where I went when I passed over at the age of two. It was paradise, there was a huge tree, and I witnessed myself in this angelic realm. I was running around with the angels. Four Archangels introduced themselves to me. Archangel Michael, Raphael, Gabriel, and Uriel. They were preparing me to meet the Divine. This vision was angelic. They said that I was growing up in this heavenly realm while I was also here on mother earth. This is what we call living in parallel Universes.

The Akashic Records are the sacred recordings of all our thoughts, words, intentions, and actions in the ether. It is a living library of our soul's vibrations. It is interactive as we create our own life here on mother earth. The wisdom in accessing our records is that we can understand our blockages, karma, and lessons in life. We recreate a new template for our blueprint. We become empowered and transcend our victim story.

I am so passionate about this teaching and how it transformed my life from being a nurse for 27 years and had become an author of 3 books.

My first book, Universal Conscious Self, is about how to tap into your essence. My second book, Ions of Manifestation, is about how to manifest your heart's desires and soul's purpose. I'm currently publishing my third book, Cosmic Soul, on how to access your Akashic Records and heal the wounds of your soul.

I feel like we are at a crossroads in our collective awakening. Darkness seems to be in our collective, arising for us to clear and heal it as we awaken from our unconscious state of being. We can navigate being more fully conscious of our existence as multidimensional beings.

As we transmute these blockages, karmic bonds, attachments, entities, hooks, cords, drains, and souls attached to us unconsciously, we can receive higher frequencies that will shift our consciousness.

The Golden Christed Light of our DNA will help activate our Higher Self and anchor this into our heart chakra, aligning with our body deva spirit. This alignment is necessary to achieve higher frequencies of Light. We are creating a formidable force field of Light within our energy system and around our etheric and auric fields. Our inner knowing, or trusting the Divine, will guide us on our light path.

No time to lose. Gather the Masters of our collective tribe that will shift the human evolution of consciousness and memories. It is time.

Receive this gift of knowledge and wisdom. The signs are all around us, and by opening our Third Eye Chakra, we will receive activations to lift the veil of separation. The universe is waiting for us as we experience this massive shift; keep your focus on what is given, our gift to the world. Pure love and Light.

We remember our Golden Light Body as we dive deeper into our unconscious. Becoming conscious of our universal self, we attune to our Higher Consciousness connected to the divine flow of love and Light. Our egoic mind loses its grasp and becomes a witness to our great transition into our Light Body. This rapid transmutation accelerates and increases our frequency of Light, thus activating our junk DNA, recoding the new template of our evolved Light Body.

This new template holds the keys for activating the new earth in our present vibrational fields. It is the return and birth of the feminine goddesses to nurture our souls back to paradise. The harmonious balance of the masculine and feminine systems will assist us in grounding our multidimensional state of being. The Sisterhood of the Rose will bring clarity, harmony, and beauty in our presence. A time to rise from any old templates of suffering. We are higher than this victim consciousness. We are the Light showers and bringers of wisdom.

The great gathering of our souls is here now.

Choose to share this Light grid around our planetary

system to vibrate higher. As our mother earth accelerates the Schumann resonance, we are being asked to increase our awareness, open our mind and heart to these transmissions of Light. Our neural pathways activate a new template and are awakened to receive the higher frequencies of Light, deeply integrating these keycodes in our dream state. Our body needs to remain still, letting go of stimulation and allowing us to regroup our scattered mind and fragmented spirit into our divine body. This temple of our incarnation is sacred. Remember to honor our vessel.

The Starseeds are being awakened to consciously anchor the Light body into our system, to function on this earthly plane fully. We can process and understand more of our existence and fully integrate all of our multidimensional states of being.

The archetypal templates of our collective will be more pronounced, releasing the survival techniques that we inherited from our human DNA, with a new model of higher consciousness, alchemical process, and morphing into this new genome. The new spectrum of rainbow Light is dispensing this grace of knowing and wisdom. There are also the arising energies from the Lemurian codes that bring harmonious, unified consciousness to our collective.

The arising and clearing of lower entities in our energetic fields is palpable. As we witness this transmutation, we are preparing the ascension of our frequency. Through a vibrational resonance of higher consciousness, we will be in a limitless and timeless state of being. The relationship of our planetary body is in alignment with the galactic movement, the dynamic momentum, and the energetic. There's a greater awareness of the planetary transition and process that the earth is experiencing.

The energies are so intense that some human beings

choose to leave this 3D state. We are given lessons of awakening and letting go of old paradigms, the old patterns, and
conditions coming from fear and survival. It is now the rise
of the collective awakening. We are blessed to witness this
transition into our new energetic template of pure love and
radiant Light. Illuminate others, rise as we create a tribe to
support us in our ascension. Be free and focus on your
radiant Light. Namaste!

ABOUT THE AUTHOR

Teza Zialcita

I was declared clinically dead as a young child and came back to life. Growing up, I have this knowing that I'm connected to the Source of all that is, aligned with the universal intelligence, mind of creation. I felt I can create what I want to be in this lifetime. But my teenage years became tumultuous, and I blamed my Higher power and family for things that didn't work out for my highest good.

As I went through my adult life, I was continually search for knowledge on how to heal me from being a sexual victim, until I connected to the studies of *Akashic Records*. That is how I've remembered where I came from. *I became an Akashic Records healer, teacher, and writer.* Through all the summation of my experiences, I became a spiritual guide. I have this gift to help open people's Book of Life, to bring clarity, understanding, and inner peace to what is blocking you from your Light.

As a wounded healer, I help you find resolution and claim back your power with situations that drained you. My mastery consists of: sexual abuse, abortion issues, grieving your child's death, family conflicts, suicide, karmic bondages, addictions, scarcity, cancer patients, death and dying. I help release, clear, and heal those unresolved and wounded aspects of your soul.

As a soul-trepreneur, I help promote other spiritual healers to be successful. My fire and passionate drive to create a tribe the *Om Healing Community Events* in Vancouver to help healers/creative artists in sharing their gifts.

My deep passion is reaching out to the orphanages in Manila, Philippines, my hometown. To give back to the poor, abandoned children. I found an affinity with their pain. As a mother who had given up my eldest son for adoption to my brother, there is a deep void in my heart. I voluntary service orphans and infuse them with healing Light. Blessings!

Teza's website : www.tezazialcita.com, email tezazialcita@gmail.com, on Facebook, www.facebook.com/tezamysticangel & YouTube channel Tezamysticangel.

~

16

MY MOTHER'S DYING WISH GAVE ME LIFE

By LILLIE LOVE

On a Friday morning in February of 2011, I woke up in my new West End apartment in Vancouver, Canada. I had arrived just over a week ago, since packing up my life in Australia. I felt my mother's energy nudging me to speak with her boyfriend.

At first, I could feel her energy was confused and unconscious. That is what a coma is, the soul going unconscious from the body. I knew that through time and space, she could receive a message from me. I explained to her Spirit about her circumstance and could take some time to decide what she wanted to do in this state.

From my perspective, she had three choices:

First, she could awaken from the coma, and her life would still be the same. She would always have Chronic fatigue, pain, and damage to her liver and lungs. Mum's body had endured much due to Hepatitis C, years of alcohol abuse, and smoking cigarettes. From there, she could choose to seek more profound healing or not.

Second, she could wake up, commit to a whole new life-style, and feel her way through all the grief and trauma she had been ignoring and repressing to reverse the disease in her body. She had already made some significant changes. She mostly did not drink since she went through a rehabili-tation center when I was 18. However, the damage to her liver had been done. She had later sought to get a liver transplant.

After going through all the tests, the doctor told her they would not approve of her liver transplant. The doctor believed her body would likely reject it anyway. The doctor then grabbed my mum's handbag and pulled out her pack of smokes, waving them in her face, saying she probably had one year to live. That was three years ago.

I further elaborated on this second choice a little more where she could have a miraculous spiritual healing, wake up completely renewed, and live a whole new life. In this new life, she would be committed to her full vitality. That option, of course, seemed a little more mystical and possibly out of her control. However, I shared my innocent curiosity, anyway. Maybe it could happen if she would ask the Divine for that grace. It never hurts to ask for a miracle.

Third, she could choose to let go of this life, this body, and return to Source.

For a few days, I felt her exploring her infinite capacity in her formless Spirit. She could be in multiple places at once. Simultaneously, she could be with me in Canada and with my brother in Melbourne, as well as with her boyfriend in Darwin. I felt her lightheartedness and sense of freedom as she flew through the cosmos, unrestricted free from a body, especially one riddled with pain and fatigue.

Rewind to a week before she went into the hospital, I was packing up the last of my home in Sydney before my move, and she called me in tears. "I'm in so much pain. Can we do that healing session now?" She was weeping. "Of course, Mumma. Let's do it now."

Only six months before this, my psychic, mediumship, and energetic senses had opened up. Beings who were no longer in human bodies were coming to me for help to resolve their ties to their former lives on Earth, so they and their loved ones could move on and be at peace. I was also experiencing being able to support the living to heal their physical ailments and emotional turmoil. Of course, I offered to do some healing work with my mum as she had been in physical and emotional pain for as long as I could remember. She would politely decline offers for healing by answering each time with "No, it's ok." I would respectfully let it go.

Honestly, I did not know what I was going to do. I had done some in-person practice sessions with friends and my boyfriend to place my hands on their bodies. I helped ghosts let go of resentment, grief, and guilt so they could move into forgiveness, which always was the antidote to being stuck in limbo. However, I questioned, "What was I going to do with my mum on a video call?"

I started by acknowledging that we were mother and daughter, and for this time, we would put all identifications of our relationship to the side and just be two human beings. Next, I imagined my hands lightly touching her feet while opening to whatever messages were coming through me.

We talked about all the Catholic guilt she still carried from her upbringing even though she had left the religion back in college in the '70s. We talked about how the beliefs she had formed as a young feminist supported and thwarted her in different ways. We talked about how her heart broke when my father left two decades before.

As I moved up to her liver and abdomen, a question came through

"Could you choose to put yourself first, be kind to you, and choose what was right for you, no matter what?"

She replied immediately, "No! No, I could not do that! That would be selfish, and people would judge me." We dug a little deeper to find out who these "people" were. It turns out it was herself. She was her most prominent judge. She always had been.

I asked, "What if we all love you no matter what? What if we support you in putting yourself first? Could you at least consider being kind to you and choosing what is right for you?" My mum took it in for a few moments. "Well, then, maybe I could." We took some long breaths. We cleared a lot of old stuff. It had been about an hour, and she was exhausted.

As we closed the container of healing we were working in, I said, "Mum, I can't speak for anyone else...I can only speak for me. I would not judge you. Whatever you choose is your choice. I want you to take care of yourself. Whatever you need is what I want."

She thanked me and remarked on how tired I must be after doing the session with her. Conversely, I noticed I felt more invigorated than ever before our call! She told me, "You have a gift!" She also expressed that she was forever grateful for me. I asked her if she wanted me to come to see her before I flew back to Canada. She said, "no" and not to worry.

Back to that rainy morning in Canada, when I woke up feeling her energy, I knew she wanted me to talk to her partner.

I immediately got on the call that evening just as he returned home from being with mum in the hospital. He began crying and said, "I don't know if she's going to make it, Lil." I shared with him the story of my last conversation with mum when we did the healing session. I told him about the question that had come to me. I wanted to ask her, and I was concerned with how mum would respond out of fear of being judged.

I told him what I told my mum at the end of our call, that no matter what she chose, I would not judge her for putting herself first. He replied, "I wouldn't judge her either, even if she chose to leave this life." We both took some deep breaths and cried. One minute later, his phone rang. It was the news of her passing.

This truth vibrated through the ethers. My mum was gone. She put herself first and was kind to herself. She chose what was right for her. I heard her whisper, "You gave me my dying wish, darling, to be free of self-judgment and shame."

After Therese's soul took flight, it was still a couple of years before I could even begin to look at the pain I had carried since childhood. I had not given myself space to grieve all of the experiences I was harboring in my nervous system, and I realized that part of me felt that my only purpose was to save my mum. Now that she was gone, I was not sure what I was supposed to do on Earth.

When there was nowhere else to go with my pain, I finally took my own medicine. I chose to put myself first–to be kind to me before the pain became unbearable and the diagnosis terminal. I sought every kind of healing modality possible and began to unravel the complicated stress and trauma that was still playing out in my life. Slowly, I began to shift my worldview from fear to love. Consequently, my sense of self transformed from one of shame to one of self-acceptance.

Therese was one of my greatest teachers. She helped me see that I am a healer. I am here to bring a message of compassion. That compassion starts with me. It also begins with you.

The question is, "When will you choose to be kind to you?"

ABOUT THE AUTHOR

Lillie Love

Lillie is a Feminine Empowerment Coach, Writer, Speaker, and Leader.

She amplifies women's process of reclaiming their Sovereignty in all capacities - sexually, emotionally, financially, creatively, and relationally.

Her gift for Somatic cellular healing as a guide for others is — on an individual and collective level -- to get out of their heads and into their bodies, where their peace, pleasure, power, purpose, and prosperity lives.

This work has saved Lillie's life. Discovering Tantra, Yoga, Life Coaching, Somatic, and Energy Work on her path to healing and overcoming sexual trauma, complex-PTSD, toxic anger, addiction, and codependency. It was a gift that she could not help but want to share with the world. Lillie transmits her knowledge from a deep place of compassion and empathy.

She stands for honoring our Great Mother Earth and restoring, healing, and evolving the equilibrium of Feminine and Masculine dynamics within and between all human beings.

∾

17

STARSEED INITIATION AND AWAKENING

By LALITAH SUNRA

I was in my twenties lying at my friend's garden, enjoying the sun and the smell of green grass and sweet flowers – suddenly, I heard myself say, "I have to work with love." Not sure if it is about self-love or intimate relationship?

I was in several broken relationships that were near impossible to fix. From alcohol, insecurities, and not being seen, I had enough! Never again.

The universe was giving me a possibility, and I decided to listen. I had fears, and I had to surrender to it. As soon as I did that, things changed. I mustered my strength and determination to change my life. I distanced myself from people and situations and moved inwards. I realized that what I once called love was not the real love I knew now. And what I labeled hate was not hate and so on and so forth. They were my old beliefs.

When I saw that everything I thought and believed to be real, then not, I took a period in my life to cleanse my body-mind-soul connection.

As my emotions turned upside down, I reviewed and redefined my feelings and beliefs. I started to read self-help books to get answers to my questions. Being all alone in my journey, I began to feel increasingly sensitive to my environment. I stopped going to party, drinking alcohol, smoking cigarettes, and cleansed myself. I thought I am being rearranged from the inside-out, unwrapping what I once heard and seen. That part of me that covered it all up to behave I belonged could no longer continue to be in denial. It just could not be any different. Yet, I felt even more alienated to the world I once knew. It was a challenging time.

Before all that, the buzzing started in my hands, and sudden attacks of migraine came. I had no clue what was going on – except it felt amazing when this buzzing came to me. It was as if energy took over my entire body. At that time, I did not have a clue what it was. I did not share it with others. But one friend whom I was sharing my findings suddenly said – "you seem different, something happened to you." She was right, the buzzing had started again, and the energy was even more potent than the first time.

She said, "If you can feel it in your hands now, then try to put them on me. Let's see what happens." The energy became more robust and bubblier, and as I placed my hands over her, she could feel the energy from my hands into her body. She could also feel it tickling the inside of her belly. We both started laughing like crazy, and something was set free in us. This was different than anything else we had experienced.

Later we found out that where the energy had tickled her the most was through the little fetus in her womb. She was pregnant, and the baby responded to our playfulness. This buzzing in my hands leads me to become a Reiki Master. It taught me how to use this energy. And later, I took Energy Healing training, which is based on Heart openings and Christ energy. That was when I learned to work with Love.

This experience was the first time I felt being pulled by the universe into the next step towards my path. I have had several of those experiences since then. I get drawn or pulled into something I would not have chosen "by myself," and following these pulls had always led me into the most amazing new discoveries.

At that time, I had opened my business in healing and coaching. I was having fun working with this newly found energy work, but I still felt it did not entirely clear my unwanted ways. It continued to resemble the old way I had chosen to get away from. I got well paid by clients, but I was not working with "love" as I felt I should.

In 2011, I began to be pulled again, very strongly this time, by an irrepressible force to just let go without knowing. It was towards India. I had no idea why because I never really wanted to go there. Since I did not travel for quite some time outside Europe, I decided to practice by visiting some friends who were sailing in the Caribbean at that time – so I sailed with them for a few weeks. It was clear when I came home, that I would travel again.

At that time, I began to get powerful and clear messages in my meditations. In one of them, I was told to go to the local church. I did not know why, so I ignored it, until the inner voice came back and said, "GO TO THE CHURCH!" So, I left what I was doing and went to the church. I told them what happened in the meditation and so I came. The woman I talked to get all excited and said they had a spiritual profile in their church, and maybe I could do meditations there. After a long talk with the priest that day, I suddenly had an appointment to provide regular meditations for Mother Earth in the church.

During this period, I was still under a meaningful change in my life. A lot happened with my whole being and belief of who I was and who I am becoming.

I used to listen a lot to Deva Premal and Miten – to carry me through and soothe my being. For me, they mirrored the love in me that I needed to feel the love inside. And they reflected a healthy and very loving relationship for others too. The next call I got was to go on holiday singing with them in Corfu that summer. As for me, who never could sing, I only did it when I was alone with my cat. Poor girl.

I was still feeling the need to clear the dark side of my old ways, but this experience turned it around. At Corfu, for the first time, I met a group of people where I felt I belonged. A connection where I could share heart to heart. I had never encountered such open, heartfelt people. I was beginning to find my tribe.

One of those days, when I went into the Buddha hall for our mantra singing, I saw a brochure lying, showing that Deva and Miten were going to be in a festival in Rishikesh India to celebrate 11.11.11. - I took the brochure and thought, "This is my ticket to India."

It was the last evening of the group and Deva, Miten and Manose. It held an open afternoon where we could just go around and talk with them as they signed their CD´s. I had a talk with Miten. I can't remember now what it was all about, but suddenly he said to me, "Why don't you come to Rishikesh in November?" I was so surprised, I said, "I just took your brochure and thought why not! I will go to Rishikesh in November," and he said, "You'll see!" - and then it was settled. I was going to Rishikesh in November. I had heard India's call.

When I got back home, I started packing my apartment. I knew I was going for an indefinite time. I was done living at my place, other places were calling. India was calling, and who knew after that? But something held me back from purchase the airplane ticket. I had the date in Rishikesh, and I had recommendations for other places to go to. I had a friend who would also go with me to the festival. So, why am I not buying the ticket? Again, I asked in my meditation: "Do I really have to go to India or what?"

In my meditation, I was shown that I was crossing a bridge over a river in India. There was a town on the other side. At the riverbank was a man sitting in bliss. When I crossed the bridge with my backpack, he got up and met me at the end of the bridge. He greeted me by putting his forehead towards mine, and I felt my third eye lit up. He said, "There you are." I said, "Who are you?" He said, "You will know when it's time." So off I went to buy my ticket. I got many more hints soon after. My India experience led me to my soul mate, my love. He was in a tantra group and greeted me by putting our foreheads together. It tickled my third eye, and I knew he was my soul mate.

I am now living love and sharing it with the world by opening myself to my own authentic Being, Healing, Art, and living my life fully. The most valuable lesson I learned was in loving myself, I attracted and mirrored my mate into my life and found my path to Love.

Starseed Sayings:

"This planet needs as many of you as possible to create a
shift now occurring."
— **Lee Harris**

ABOUT THE AUTHOR

Lalitah Sunra

Lalitha is a truth-seeker, dedicating her life to follow her truth, help others get the courage, unblock one's path to follow their own truth. She offers lineage clearing supported by seven years of meditations. She gets visions, connects to mother earth and sky through rituals, and uses creativity to express experiences from other realms. She believes in supporting your purpose to unfold your truth and walk your path. Gifted to zoom into seeing things about issues others cannot see from a Soul Level, she communicates knowledge to understand your present experience and reconnects you to your True voice and clear blockages. Caring and sensitive energy healer, who could sense the collective field - the fields of Oneness, where she feels the presence of life works through her.

She discovered her healing abilities as gifts from the universe during her search for philosophical, psychological, esoteric, and spiritual topics. Had visitations from other realms but never knew of her power.

Buzzing in her hands - she felt was very loving and insisting, led her to a reiki healer, Energy Healing education, Osho Therapist Training, Intuitive Painting Guide training, Soul Art Guide training, Tantric training, and practiced healing arts for more than 16 years. Later created her modality called Ascension Touch and Primordial Language Healing modality. Meditations for seven years supported her work.

"There is nothing more satisfying than seeing authentic people show up. Because when one stops hiding behind conditioned beliefs and habits and steps up into their light to share their truth, it feels real. And the funny thing is — that when we start sharing from a place of real-life experience and transmute it, we can get what we dream of. We have to overcome the fear and step out. That is the way to gain our power."

Lalitha will lovingly support you in unfolding your true self and step into the next level of your ascension process so you can live your Magic.

～

18

CONTACT IN THE DESERT

By MICHAEL PESTANO

For as long as I can remember, I knew I was different. An alien stranded in a time and place, not my own. A wanderer, a hitchhiker, a space gypsy was traipsing through time and space across multi-dimensions.

Born into a country within a family, culture, religion, and society steeped in an uneasy mix of fear, love, and subservience. Yes, that's precisely how I came into this reality on 02/11/1967 in a hospital in the Philippines. Those were tumultuous times with the Vietnam War in full tilt and the Philippines itself about to be shackled by an iron-fisted dictator in a few years. It was the height of Flower Power and free-flowing psychedelic drugs. It, too, was the height of the Cold War between the US and the Soviet Union. The Doomsday clock is counting down to Armageddon. What a time to be born!

I distinctly remember myself standing in my crib in the dark as a toddler alone, staring at a full moon and crying because I hated the stifling nervous energies crackling around me. I dreaded the visits of strange people, men and women dressed in black and carrying rosaries and anointing me on the head with water. I was told that if I misbehaved, a headless priest would come to visit me in the dark while sleeping and take me to hell. That explains why that trauma stayed with me, and I was terrified of the night until I was thirteen years old.

As I grew up, this feeling of disconnect grew even more energetic, and I felt so alone and out of place. I felt many energies and emotions, not my own, and sometimes voices in my head in a language so foreign. I'd find myself lost in a daydream many times while in school. I was an artist, a painter, and a writer at that time. What I drew was not the usual run-of-the-mill stuff. I sketched in pencil many cityscapes, not of this earth. Monoliths, glass and crystal buildings, flying vehicles, all shapes and sizes. The stars and the planets were my other favorites to draw. I'd draw galaxies and imagined them as my star charts. I drew figures that were not human in various shapes and sizes. I yearned for the stars and felt so disconnected from my parents. I kept calling out to the Universe to take me back home. But no one answered. Many nights I cried myself to sleep homesick for a place so far, far away.

Resigned to my fate, I tolerated the regular Sunday visits to church and fearfully followed the teachings. It didn't help that many religious people come and go in and out of our house and "remind" me how important it was to be a good Christian Catholic boy. Even at that young age, it did not sit well with me that there was a God I was forced to love and worship or else. A God was supposed to be benevolent and full of love, but there would be hell to pay if I got on his wrong side. A God separated from me.

If I were really misbehaving and disobeyed his laws, a

particular red-skinned, cloven-hoofed demon with a trident would appear and take me with him to his fiery kingdom and burn for all eternity. Given that option, I grudgingly submitted myself to indoctrination. Constant physical and emotional punishment over the years can sway the mind of a twelve-year-old.

For the next two decades, I trained and studied in the finest academies of higher learning. I lived that rich, gilded, protected, and insulated life for the most part. There was the occasional time my original programming would try to surface but would then be brutally suppressed by the Dark Side's mind game tactics.

I was in college at that time in 1985, and I wrote a short story about myself as an astronaut with my pet dog on a mission towards Jupiter. Upon entering the gaseous atmosphere, something happened, and there was an electrostatic reaction that transformed both my dog and me into light forms. We could communicate with each other through telepathy, and we were visited by five light beings, each with its specific color. Red, green, white, violet, and blue were the colors of these beings. They told my astronaut character and my dog that we did not need our limited bodies as this was our pure form. God is everywhere and in everything. The real evolution of humanity was at hand, and it was time to wake up and embrace our God selves.

I wrote that story in two hours of writing in class and submitted it to my college professor. The next day, the professor asked to see me after class. He asked me where the heck did I get that outlandish yet beautifully written story. He gave me a B+ for its originality and creativity, but he said if I had not claimed to be God along with my dog, I would have gotten an A+. I remember when I wrote that story, everything just came out of my heart and soul and flowed for the next couple of hours. Then I went back into deep hibernation.

Living in amnesia until I was 44 years old, I was breaking down in body and mind. Life signs flickering, I cried out and sent an emergency beacon. The Universe sent me its cosmic equivalent of Navy Seals headed by a powerful Galactic Goddess, Radhaa Nilia, and a Lemurian Shaman, Maya the Shaman. For good measure, a fiery and charismatic medicine man was included along the way with two young tech wizards. My version of Guardians of the Galaxy guided me out of hell and transformed me. I went back deep inside the shadows and recovered that frightened, lost child to reintegrate him and fully embrace my true self. I reclaimed my power and recovered my soul fragments across infinity. This time, love, gratitude, and forgiveness would be the new norm. My mission accomplished. It was time for the next one.

I got my new mission orders in 2015 while visiting Sedona, Arizona, for the third time. Sedona has a world-wide reputation as a sacred and spiritual cathedral without walls. I specifically set an intention for myself at the famous vortexes, Airport Mesa, Bell Rock, and Cathedral Rock. The Airport Mesa vortex blends both masculine and feminine energies. Bell Rock was masculine, and Cathedral Rock is for the divine feminine.

I love to hike in nature, and the first trail I tackled was Bell Rock. I immediately felt the powerful masculine energy the moment I stepped out of the car. I went for a short hike in the stifling heat and felt a firm yet familiar energetic presence emanating from high above the sky. I could barely make out this cigar-shaped shiny metallic spacecraft hover for a few seconds. It was enough time for me to grab my smartphone and snap a picture as it disappeared in a flash.

The image on my phone was barely the size of a pinhead. It was enough.

After that, I excitedly rushed back to my car and drove to Cathedral Rock. By then, there were probably a couple of hours of daylight left. I hurriedly parked and scrambled past the dry riverbed towards the entrance to the trail. I had barely walked a few hundred meters when the air turned dense and still. It was like time had stopped, and there was this eerie quietness all around me. I turned my gaze towards the opening, which perfectly framed the setting sun. I felt the warm and soothing Light hit my face, and I froze. I could not move at all. Then I heard this gentle, soothing, and hypnotic female voice in my head saying, "It is time. You are ready now. It's your sacred mission. Will you accept?" Without thinking, I just said yes. I let my heart guide me.

At the same time, my memory banks were flashing back to that time I wrote that astronaut story. I could see those five different colored light-beings floating in front of me, plus my long-lost first pet dog. That dog in the story was based on my first pet named Snookie, and I loved her so much. She got lost when she was a puppy, and I was so heartbroken. Now she was back as this light form yet recognizable, and she told me she had been with me all along. She was my spirit guide from the stars and back on the mission with me. The five beings with her I recognized as my angels, Michael, Gabriel, Uriel, Metatron, and Raphael. They told me they were part of this mission. They were part of this most massive Galactic team of Light ever put together. My Earth team was waiting. The Awakening Starseeds team is now here and ready. It's my family, and I'm coming home.

Starseed Saying:

The Universe and the light come through me.

— **Rumi**

ABOUT THE AUTHOR

Michael Pestano

Michael Pestano is a health coach, motivational speaker, business consultant for organic foods and supplement companies. A certified fitness trainer specializing in sports and exercise nutrition and weight loss devoted to complete wellness and a holistic preventive approach to illness. He has been in the natural health and wellness industry since 1998 and is dedicated to sharing with the world the benefits of living a healthy lifestyle in mind, body, and spirit.

His first two health books. I Am Enough - Healing A Broken Body and Into the Shadows, after healing type 2 diabetes, autoimmune hepatitis, and overcoming severe obesity. These two near-death experiences changed his life. Awakened and stunned by this experience, he began an intensive journey involving self-inquiry and discovery, culminating in creating his own mind, body, and spirit transformation programs.

Finding natural solutions to incurable autoimmune conditions, he committed to sharing and spreading the wisdom of health: mind, body, and spirit. Two new books coming out namely, Infinite Abundance of the Universe and 90 Days to Transformation.

His podcast, I Am Enough with Iron Eagle Mike, is available on 10 different platforms, including Apple iTunes, Spotify, and Google Podcasts. Learn about the amazing power of your Thoughts, Intentions, positivity, affirmations, and mindset, self-empowerment in mind, body, and spirit. Sharing the power of nutrition, exercise, and mental reprogramming towards a strong and limitless human being. Conversations about alternative healing, energy healing, spirituality, and other topics outside the box. On YouTube channel, you can also find Mike I Am Enough TV with Iron Eagle Mike, on LinkedIn as Mike Pestano, and Instagram @ironeaglemike88. Mike also conducts health workshops online and through many local health and wellness events in Southern California.

Websites:
www.ironeaglemike.com
www.michaelpestano.arbonne.com
www.hempworx.com/ironeaglemike
https://www.amazon.com/shop/influencer-ea7faadd

∾

19

I AM MY FATHER'S DAUGHTER

By ABIGAIL DIAZ JUAN

As I prepare to birth my purpose and destiny into the world, it took a visit to Maya The Shaman, a Lemurian Code Healer. My intention was to put together the pieces of the puzzle in my life. She asked me to write a chapter in "Awakening Starseeds, Shattering Illusions."

You see, I was born in Kabul, Afghanistan, of Filipino parents with the defining years of my childhood spent in Kandahar. It was the time of the Afghan monarchy, a few years before the Russians were to change the destiny of Afghanistan from a peaceful paradise to the war-torn nation of today. The idyllic Afghanistan that I remember sadly no longer exists today.

My Father was Ilocano, and my mother is Visayan, two very different regions in the Philippines. They needed the universal language, Tagalog, to even speak to each other.

My father courted my mother for 11 years, proposed several times, and each time she said no. Since my father was working as an expatriate in Afghanistan as the communications engineer for the US Ambassador at the time, he could only court my mother each time he came back to the Philippines for vacation every two years. When she finally said yes, he didn't waste any time getting married, and their honeymoon was spent on the plane being transported from the only life she knew in the Philippines. They arrived in a foreign country where my mother found out she was the first-ever Filipina female and wife allowed to live there at the time.

Afghanistan at that history of time was considered too hazardous for families. Typically only men were allowed to work there, leaving behind their spouses and families back in their home countries. My father broke protocol by bringing his young wife back with him. My inexperienced mother had to learn in real-time, without any preparation or in-country support, how to live her daily life within the unknown world of the expatriate enclave community in a Muslim country. This was to be a theme that I would take on in my own adulthood as both a Filipina female and as a young entrepreneur, breaking barriers of entry into unknown worlds and adjusting on the fly to ever-changing circumstances.

Today's large overseas Filipino global population is primarily due to President Ferdinand Marcos exporting Filipino human talents to work in various industries world-wide. At the time, he made Filipino talent and labor more affordable and attractive to governments around the world and multinational organizations than hiring their own nationals. Initially, my father expected to build his career in the Philippine Navy, which had sent him to Treasure Island in the San Francisco Bay Area to train as a communications engineer. A chance conversation with a relative upon his return to Manila changed his trajectory from a known and expected life in the Navy to one filled with adventure and exploration as an expatriate working for the US State Department in Afghanistan, handling all communications for the US Ambassador. His job took him all over the country, including clandestinely setting up American listening posts along the Russian-Afghan border during the Cold War. As a field engineer traveling throughout the country, my father lived his purpose and thrived at it.

I was born into this amazing juxtaposition of a modern and yet biblically foreign environment. I grew up as a member of the tight-knit Filipino community enclosed within a broader expatriate community that consisted of families from at least 25 countries serving multiple multinational organizations, NGOs, and international governmental agencies during the Cold War era. It was much later that I realized that my childhood was a privileged life within a very unique environment during an extraordinary time in history. It was a microcosmic experience within a macrocosmic global environment filled with collaborative love, absent of the socially divisive fear that we live in today.

Unknowing of the path ahead of me but ready to take it on, I was born with the assistance of the US Ambassador's doctor and the Afghan Queen's midwife. Named Abigail, I emerged into our 3D world with gusto.

My childhood was spent being my "Father's Daughter." He and I enjoyed a special father-daughter relationship. He taught me how to do all the outdoor pastimes that a father teaches his son typically. As a tomboy, I learned the pleasures of fishing, hunting, driving, mountain climbing, and outdoor exploration. I learned how to solve problems tinkering mechanically and constructively beside him in his workshop. And I learned the pleasures of ballroom dancing by standing on his feet as a young girl dancing to the music at the many various parties we attended. It is from him teaching me how to draw on a pad, use a typewriter to write stories, and shoot pictures with his Cannon camera that I developed my creative and artistic side. My mother, to her chagrin, could not get me to cook, sew, embroider, or attend to any household duties that any self-respecting female at that time usually did. After all, I was my father's daughter, and we had servants to do all the household stuff anyway.

They say that the Universe will always show humans the other side of a good life so that we can know what LOVE truly is from the context of juxtaposition, the view from the other side – where the dark absence of love and light exists.

Everything changed for me in my relationship with my father when we immigrated to the United States at the height of the Cold War. The Russians invaded Afghanistan right after we left. My father's next diplomatic assignment ended abruptly when Iran ceased to be a secular nation as the Grand Ayatollah came into power. With international political conflict rife in the region, my mother decided it was time to move to San Francisco, California.

It is here in this urban society within the public school system of California that I was introduced to socially-induced fear, the juxtaposition to the communal unconditional love that I was accustomed to in Afghanistan. Picked on by a school bully in San Francisco and initiated into conformity by the gangs in San Jose by merely being different was a negative introduction to modern society for me. It was the equivalent of abruptly waking up from a cozy night's sleep by the contact of a bucket of cold water thrown onto my face.

Like my mother's abrupt and rough introduction to Afghanistan, I had to learn how to quickly survive in an urban world ruled by social predators in California. Unlike the expatriate community in Afghanistan, where multi-diversity was the common thread that linked us all and knitted us together, here, one's differences were what separated one another from the communal group. At the same time, social conformity was enforced through fear-induced isolation. It was how I got accepted.

My father did not fare any better in this impersonal environment. Taken away from his beloved outdoors and trapped into a desk job at a high-tech company, he was out of his natural environment, and his soul began to die as he struggled to take care of his family in this new artificially controlled environment.

A gentle, humble, and quiet man, my dad became exposed to overt discrimination as both a minority immigrant and a professional worker. His vast field engineering experience from Afghanistan did not matter in a large pool of desk-oriented credentialed talent in Silicon Valley. And his lack of financial ambition and corporate expertise proved to be his downfall. Categorized as a highly paid specialist lacking managerial experience, he was often included in the first wave of corporate layoffs during the turbulent times of the '90s in Silicon Valley. Upon the request of his family, my father retired early. His wings clipped, he reverted to his childhood past growing up on a farm and found soulful solace in his own backyard garden. Over the years, he became the go-to expert for others on organic farming long before the concept became popular.

However, the death of his career purpose and the failure to provide for his family built an internal rage that consistently ate away at his soul. Introduced to fear-driven conformity in the United States, my father lacked the understanding of financial investment and money in general. As the head of our household, unfortunately, he approached every potential financial opportunity to get ahead and prosper with tremendous fear and trepidation. Money discussions always triggered his sense of powerlessness about his incapability to take care of his family and offended his Filipino macho male sensibilities. Sadly, as in many families, his wife often bore the brunt of his emotional outrage at the hand dealt him by society.

On the other hand, my mother was brought up in a business-minded family, so her approach was more optimistic and pragmatic. However, growing up in a beachside barangay in the province of Cebu did not prepare her for the big city life of high finance, investments, and wealth management. Her financial knowledge was limited to tight budgeting and savings in a bank. It was within this financial approach to life that my relationship with my father changed and became adversarial in contrast to the allied supportive companionship we shared in my childhood. "They say that muscles grow when practiced upon something firm and hard." My financial acumen developed against my father's fear of financial risk.

As a young adult, incapable of utilizing my resources for myself, my father's consistent rejection of the multitude of opportunities I brought to the family (based simply on his fear of expanding into the unknown), created a tremendous frustration and determination within me to prove that I could do better and grow beyond my familial circumstances. Inherently, I knew I was born to be more than just ordinary. After all, I was escorted into this world by the US Ambassador's doctor and the Afghan Queen's midwife!

In my childhood's many mountain climbing exertions where I would survey the vast plains of the Hindu Kush mountain range atop my favorite ledge for hours on end, I intuitively knew that I was meant to do something special in this world and that special something included handling large flows of money and wealth. The Midas Touch energy was alive and well within me, and I just needed to know how to bring it out into the world to accomplish my mission and purpose in this incarnation.

Against this backdrop of paternal resistance, unbeknownst to my father, my mother managed to support my entrepreneurial endeavors quietly; and, over the years, stayed as my silent partner and steady supporter through my many trials and errors as I climbed up the entrepreneurial ladder. My entire climb to the summit of the mountain to ultimately become a venture capitalist with a multi-billion-dollar fund was initiated in the mid-'80s by a 10,000-dollar loan from my mother to help me start my first entrepreneurial business in marketing communications.

It was both arduous and filled with ego-driven effort to climb up my professional ladder. I had something to prove, and I was determined to succeed. I learned how to be a samurai warrior as I studied the habits of those who inhabited this international finance, marketing, and business incubation landscape. I learned all about power, control, and money. Unbeknownst to me, having long forgotten about my childhood musings of what I would become in life, I was internally growing, remembering, and transforming. All in preparation for my destined work -- one that was to be spiritual in nature.

I may not necessarily agree with what my soul thinks is right for my trajectory onto my destiny's path. But I have come to understand now that the Universe and my soul determine my way in life.

Over the years, this Great Universe of ours has prepared me for my destined work by pivoting me into vastly different situations, thereby catapulting me into new, ever-evolving circumstances to expand my consciousness continuously.

To be continued (See me on Volume 2)

In love and light!

Mabuhay!

ABOUT THE AUTHOR

Abigail Diaz Juan

Abigail Diaz Juan reached her pinnacle of business success as a Venture Capitalist years ago, managing her very own multi-billion-dollar venture fund in Silicon Valley. When her destiny came knocking, it triggered a spontaneous kundalini awakening disguised as a debilitating illness, forcing her to retire from that successful life.

Her intense spiritual journey introduced her to a new paradigm of living: "Before our identity is defined by society, and before our gender defines us, we are first and foremost a human being -- a member species on this great planet Earth of ours, inherently powerful in our own right with our own individual destiny as our sovereign birthright."

Today, as an international speaker, venture capitalist, spiritual entrepreneur, and women's empowerment advocate, Abigail Diaz Juan, author of "How Me Found I: Mastering the Art of Pivoting Gracefully Through Life," introduces us to a revolutionary approach to rediscovering the self, redefining the way life is meant to be lived, and revitalizing personal potential and purpose.

Abby can be reached at: www.AbigailDiazJuan.com

~

RADHAA PUBLISHING HOUSE

ABOUT Radhaa Publishing House

Radhaa Publishing House is a holistic publishing company that focuses on helping heart-centered, mind-expanding, truth-telling authors get their work out into the world.

Our focus is on collaborative book series and memoirs. We thrive on supporting our authors throughout this journey, empowering them to step into their divine and an authentic voice while sharing their truth with the world. We especially celebrate cultural diversity from around the world. We believe in weaving international voices to come together.

How are we different?

Many collaborative publishing companies bundle the authors together so that they don't receive individual credit and acknowledgment. We make sure each Author is seen and heard and can be found easily. This has led to authors telling us that they have received more traffic on their websites and more business and clients. In a sense, each of the Starseeds series is also a Starseeds Directory highlighting their unique offerings. This has been a win-win for the authors. It's an extra gift that our publishing company generously offers them as we frame their gifts beautifully to be seen.

∼

Here's what our authors have said about working with us:

"I felt totally supported. The best bit was feeling like being part of a loving family who wants you to be your best, do your best, and is there for you every step of the way. It also boosted my confidence as a writer. The collaborative nature of the project also made it way more fun than doing things alone".

\- Arrameia, Prague

———

"Visibility was a big piece of me coming out of the spiritual closet, and I felt that Radhaa Publishing House has a high energy and integrity level. Both of which are important for lightworkers and starseeds and our message. The curators are all Starseeds themselves, and Radhaa Publishing House created this wonderful opportunity for many others to see. I felt that they put their whole heart into making this happen even before, during, and after. It was a project that was totally supportive that made me feel safe to share myself and my story."

\- Lalitah, Turkey

———

"My story was edited by Radhaa Publishing House, and let me tell you, it put me in tears! They made it better than the way I originally wrote and submitted it while keeping my story and voice true to its events. I read it, and tears just flowed because it was so good!"
- Cristal, Florida

————

"It is a great supportive community, and they let you, Shine, BRIGHTLY! The best part is you get to share your story in a way that will bring some healing to yourself and other Starseeds. What stood out the most is their passion to get people to recognize their path of healing, enlightenment, and passion for a life towards full expression through storytelling."
- Raziel, California

————

"It was wonderful to work with Radhaa Publishing House. I saw the effort and perseverance the whole team has and the support system you have for all the authors. I have matured as an author from this experience. I was so inspired after writing my chapter in this book, Awakening Starseeds, that I wrote an entire book called The Great Awakening because I was deeply moved by writing with Radhaa Publishing House."
- Leshara, Philippines

————

Awakening Starseeds BOOK SERIES

At Radhaa Publishing House, we are highly involved in the entire process and work personally with the authors to navigate authorship challenges.

Our authors are heart-centered, soul-driven, and ready to manifest their legacy. We acknowledge the courage and strength it takes to step out into the public eye, and our team is here to support you all the way.

Creating a book is a tedious process and requires persistence, patience, and perspective. There are many moving parts of the book that needs attention, and our team knows how to work hard to ensure we are able to come through with flying colors for the final date of our release.

————

If you're a Starseed with a compelling story to share with the world, dream of being a published author and wish to be a part of the Awakening Starseeds family, reach out to us.
"Be that change you wanted to be in our world!"

———

By sharing your story with lessons learned, you anchor the positive teachings for others to aspire in their becoming. The valuable lessons you possess are genuinely your gifts to our changing 3D reality.
Step into your voice and be heard now! When you become an author of Awakening Starseeds, you empower yourself in a way you may have never experienced before. At least, that's what our authors tell us.

<u>YOUR LITERARY WORK</u>

No other publishing company offers you
in-house support the way that Radhaa Publishing House
does. Join us in the next Volume of Awakening Starseeds.

Your legacy awaits! So, claim your author power now!

———

Contact us at:

Radhaa Publishing House Info:
www.RadhaaPublishingHouse.com
Email: RadhaaPublishing@gmail.com

TO OUR READERS:

Dear Starseeds readers,
If you like our Awakening Starseeds stories, please support
us by leaving a review online.
You can find us at Amazon.com

———

We cannot do this without your support!
Share this journey with us!
Sincerely,
Radhaa Publishing House Team

**"Awakening Starseeds, Beyond The Stargate Volume 2" is
coming this summer 2021**

To order a signed copy of Awakening Starseeds Volume 1 or
2, visit our online store: https://radhaanilia.net/shop/

Thank you!

COMING SOON!
This Summer 2021

Awakening Starseeds, Stories Beyond The Stargate

Volume 2

———————

To order a signed copy of Awakening Starseeds
Visit our Online Store
https://radhaanilia.net/shop/

Lightning Source UK Ltd.
Milton Keynes UK
UKHW042104031122
411597UK00001B/185